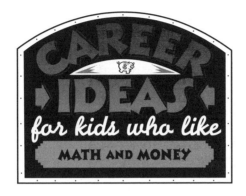

CAREER
IDEAS
for kids who like
MATH AND MONEY

THE CAREER IDEAS FOR KIDS SERIES

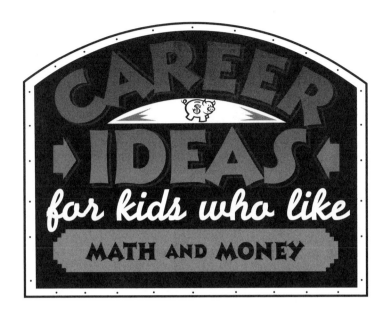

Second Edition

DIANE LINDSEY REEVES
with
LINDSEY CLASEN

Illustrations by
NANCY BOND

Ferguson
An imprint of Infobase Publishing

CAREER IDEAS FOR KIDS WHO LIKE MATH AND MONEY, Second Edition

Copyright © 2007 by Diane Lindsey Reeves

Ferguson
An imprint of Infobase Publishing, Inc.
132 West 31st Street
New York NY 10001

Library of Congress Cataloging-in-Publication Data

Reeves, Diane Lindsey, 1959–
    Career ideas for kids who like math and money / Diane Lindsey Reeves with Lindsey Clasen; illustrations by Nancy Bond. —2nd ed.
        p. cm — (The career ideas for kids series)
    Rev. ed. of: Career ideas for kids who like math. c2000; Career ideas for kids who like money. c2001.
    Includes bibliographical references and index.
    ISBN-13: 978-0-8160-6545-5 (hc : alk. paper)
    ISBN-10: 0-8160-6545-4 (hc : alk. paper)
    1. Finance—Vocational guidance—Huvenile literature. 2. Financial services industry—Vocational guidance—Juvenile literature. 3. Business—Vocational guidance—Juvenile literature. 4. Mathematics—Vocational guidance—Juvenile literature. I. Clasen, Lindsey. II. Bond, Nancy, ill. III. Reeves, Diane Lindasey, 1959– Career ideas for kids who like math. IV. Reeves, Diane Lindsey, 1959– Career ideas for kids who like Money. V. Title.
    HG173.8.R437 2007
    331.702—dc21   2007009721

Ferguson books are available at special discounts when purchased in bulk quantities for businesses, associations, institutions, or sales promotions. Please call our Special Sales Department in New York at (212) 967-8800 or (800) 322-8755.

You can find Facts On File on the World Wide Web at http://www.factsonfile.com

Original text and cover design by Smart Graphics
Illustrations by Nancy Bond

Printed in the United States of America

MP Hermitage 10 9 8 7 6 5 4 3 2 1

This book is printed on acid-free paper.

CONTENTS

ACKNOWLEDGMENTS

A million thanks to the people who took the time to share their career stories and provide photos for this book:

Peter and Cheryl Barnes
Charley Biggs
Lenore Blum
Henk-Jan Brinkman
Joe Carver
Jim Cramer
William Elsner
Whit Friese
Susan Gravely
Nishat Karimi
Ramona Mullahey
B. LaRae Orullian
Sharon Robinson
Matt Rosenberg
Cynthia Tucker

Finally, much appreciation and admiration is due to my editor, James Chambers, whose vision and attention to detail increased the quality of this project in many wonderful ways.

MAKE A CHOICE!

Choices.

You make them every day. What do I want for breakfast? Which shirt can I pull out of the dirty-clothes hamper to wear to school today? Should I finish my homework or play video games?

Some choices don't make much difference in the overall scheme of things. Face it; who really cares whether you wear the blue shirt or the red one?

Other choices are a major big deal. Figuring out what you want to be when you grow up is one of those all-important choices.

But, you say, you're just a kid. How are you supposed to know what you want to do with your life?

You're right: 10, 11, 12, and even 13 are a bit young to know exactly what and where and how you're going to do whatever it is you're going to do as an adult. But it's the perfect time to start making some important discoveries about who you are, what you like to do, and what you do best. It's a great time to start exploring the options and experimenting with different ideas. In fact, there's never a better time to mess around with different career ideas without messing up your life.

When it comes to picking a career, you've basically got two choices.

MAYBE
DEFINITELY
SOUNDS COOL
NO WAY

CHOICE A

You can be like lots of other people and just go with the flow. Float through school doing only what you absolutely have to in order to graduate, take any job you can find, collect a paycheck, and meander your way to retirement without making much of a splash in life.

Although many people take this route and do just fine, others end up settling for second best. They miss out on a meaningful education, satisfying work, and the rewards of a focused and well-planned career. That's why this path is not an especially good idea for someone who actually wants to have a life.

CHOICE B

Other people get a little more involved in choosing a career. They figure out what they want to accomplish in their lives—whether it's making a difference, making lots of money, or simply enjoying what they do. Then they find out what it takes to reach that goal, and they set about doing it with gusto. It's kind of like these people do things on purpose instead of letting life happen by accident.

Choosing A is like going to an ice cream parlor where there are all kinds of awesome flavors and ordering a single scoop of plain vanilla. Going with Choice B is more like visiting that same ice cream parlor and ordering a super duper brownie sundae drizzled with hot fudge, smothered in whip cream, and topped with a big red cherry.

Do you see the difference?

Reading this book is a great idea for kids who want to go after life in a big way. It provides a first step toward learning about careers that match your skills, values, and dreams. It will help you make the most out of your time in school and maybe even inspire you to—as the U.S. Army so proudly says—"be all that you can be."

Ready for the challenge of Choice B? If so, read the next section for instructions on how to get started.

HOW TO USE THIS BOOK

This book isn't just about interesting careers that other people have. It's also a book about interesting careers that you can have.

Of course, it won't do you a bit of good to just read this book. To get the whole shebang, you're going to have to jump in with both feet, roll up your sleeves, put on your thinking cap—whatever it takes—to help you do these three things:

☀ Discover what you do best and enjoy the most. (This is the secret ingredient for finding work that's perfect for you.)

☼ Explore ways to match your interests and abilities with career ideas.

☼ Experiment with lots of different ideas until you find the ideal career. (It's like trying on all kinds of hats to see which ones fit!)

Use this book as a road map to some exciting career destinations. Here's what to expect in the chapters that follow.

GET IN GEAR!

First stop: discover. These activities will help you uncover important clues about the special traits and abilities that make you *you*. When you are finished you will have developed a personal Skill Set that will help guide you to career ideas in the next chapter.

TAKE A TRIP!

Next stop: explore. Cruise down the career idea highway and find out about a variety of career ideas that are especially appropriate for people who like math and money. Use the Skill Set chart at the beginning of each career profile to match your own interests with those required for success on the job.

Once you've identified a career that interests you, kick your exploration into high gear by checking out some of the Web sites, library resources, and professional organizations listed at the end of each career profile. For an extra challenge, follow the instructions for the Try It Out activities.

MAKE A DETOUR THAT COUNTS!

Here's your chance to explore up-and-coming opportunities in the business world, ways to be your own boss, and careers with higher than average earning potential. You'll also get to explore careers in technology, science, and other fields in combination with your passion for numbers.

4

Just when you thought you'd seen it all, here come dozens of math and moneymaking ideas to add to the career mix. Charge up your career search by learning all you can about some of these opportunities.

DON'T STOP NOW!

Third stop: experiment. The library, the telephone, a computer, and a mentor—four keys to a successful career planning adventure. Use them well, and before long you'll be on the trail of some hot career ideas of your own.

WHAT'S NEXT?

Make a plan! Chart your course (or at least the next stop) with these career planning road maps. Whether you're moving full steam ahead with a great idea or get slowed down at a yellow light of indecision, these road maps will keep you moving forward toward a great future.

Use a pencil—you're bound to make a detour or two along the way. But, hey, you've got to start somewhere.

HOORAY! YOU DID IT!

Some final rules of the road before sending you off to new adventures.

SOME FUTURE DESTINATIONS

This section lists a few career planning tools you'll want to know about.

You've got a lot of ground to cover in this phase of your career planning journey. Start your engines and get ready for an exciting adventure!

Career planning is a lifelong journey. There's usually more than one way to get where you're going, and there are often some interesting detours along the way. But you have to start somewhere. So rev up and find out all you can about one-of-a-kind, specially designed you. That's the first stop on what can be the most exciting trip of your life!

To get started, complete the five exercises described throughout the following pages.

DISCOVER #1: WATCH FOR SIGNS ALONG THE WAY

Road signs help drivers figure out how to get where they want to go. They provide clues about direction, road conditions, and safety. Your career road signs will provide clues about who you are, what you like, and what you do best. These clues can help you decide where to look for the career ideas that are best for you.

Complete the following statements to make them true for you. There are no right or wrong answers. Jot down the response that describes you best. Your answers will provide important clues about career paths you should explore.

Please Note: If this book does not belong to you, write your responses on a separate sheet of paper.

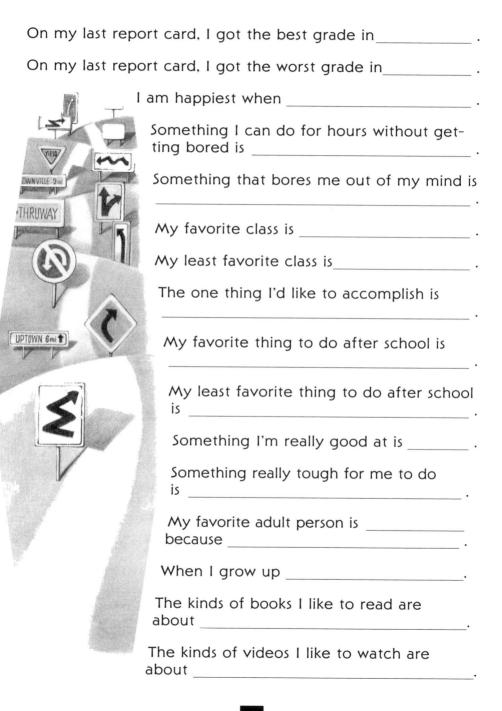

On my last report card, I got the best grade in _____ .

On my last report card, I got the worst grade in _____ .

I am happiest when _____ .

Something I can do for hours without getting bored is _____ .

Something that bores me out of my mind is
_____ .

My favorite class is _____ .

My least favorite class is_____ .

The one thing I'd like to accomplish is
_____ .

My favorite thing to do after school is
_____ .

My least favorite thing to do after school
is _____ .

Something I'm really good at is _____ .

Something really tough for me to do
is _____ .

My favorite adult person is _____
because _____ .

When I grow up _____ .

The kinds of books I like to read are
about _____ .

The kinds of videos I like to watch are
about _____ .

DISCOVER #2: RULES OF THE ROAD

Pretty much any job you can think of involves six common ingredients. Whether the work requires saving the world or selling bananas, all work revolves around a central **purpose** or reason for existing. All work is conducted somewhere, in some **place**, whether it's on the 28th floor of a city sky-scraper or on a cruise ship in the middle of an ocean. All work requires a certain **time** commitment and is performed using various types of **tools**. **People** also play an important part in most jobs—whether the job involves interacting with lots or very few of them. And, especially from where you are sitting as a kid still in school, all work involves some type of **preparation** to learn how to do the job.

Another word for these six common ingredients is "values." Each one represents important aspects of work that people value in different ways. The following activity will give you a chance to think about what matters most to you in each of these areas. That way you'll get a better idea of things to look for as you explore different careers.

Here's how the process works:

First, read the statements listed for each value on the following pages. Decide which, if any, represent your idea of an ideal job.

Next, take a look at the grid on page 16. For every value statement with which you agreed, draw its symbol in the appropriate space on your grid. (If this book doesn't belong to you, use a blank sheet of paper to draw your own grid with six big spaces.) Or, if you want to get really fancy, cut pictures out of magazines and glue them into the appropriate space. If you do not see a symbol that represents your best answer, make up a new one and sketch it in the appropriate box.

When you are finished, you'll have a very useful picture of the kinds of values that matter most to you in your future job.

PURPOSE

Which of the following statements describes what you most hope to accomplish in your future work? Pick as many as are true for you and feel free to add others.

❤	❑	I want to help other people.
💵	❑	I want to make lots of money.
★	❑	I want to do something I really believe in.
✋	❑	I want to make things.
🧠	❑	I want to use my brain power in challenging ways.
💡	❑	I want to work with my own creative ideas.
🏆	❑	I want to be very successful.
🛝	❑	I want to find a good company and stick with it for the rest of my life.
🔦	❑	I want to be famous.

Other purpose-related things that are especially important to me are

PLACE

When you think about your future work, what kind of place would you most like to do it in? Pick as many as are true for you and feel free to add others.

	❏	I want to work in a big city skyscraper.
	❏	I want to work in a shopping mall or retail store.
	❏	I want to work in the great outdoors.
	❏	I want to travel a lot for my work.
	❏	I want to work out of my own home.
	❏	I want to work for a government agency.
	❏	I want to work in a school or university.
	❏	I want to work in a factory or laboratory.

Other place-related things that are especially important to me are

GET IN GEAR!

TIME When you think about your future work, what kind of schedule sounds most appealing to you? Pick as many as are true for you and feel free to add others.		
	❏	I'd rather work regular business hours—nine to five, Monday through Friday.
	❏	I'd like to have lots of vacation time.
	❏	I'd prefer a flexible schedule so I can balance my work, family, and personal needs.
	❏	I'd like to work nights only so my days are free.
	❏	I'd like to work where the pace is fast and I stay busy all day.
	❏	I'd like to work where I would always know exactly what I'm supposed to do.
	❏	I'd like to work where I could plan my own day.
	❏	I'd like to work where there's lots of variety and no two days are alike.

Other time-related things that are especially important to me are

TOOLS

What kinds of things would you most like to work with? Pick as many as are true for you and feel free to add others.

	❑	I'd prefer to work mostly with people.
	❑	I'd prefer to work mostly with technology.
	❑	I'd prefer to work mostly with machines.
	❑	I'd prefer to work mostly with products people buy.
	❑	I'd prefer to work mostly with planes, trains, automobiles, or other things that go.
	❑	I'd prefer to work mostly with ideas.
	❑	I'd prefer to work mostly with information.
	❑	I'd prefer to work mostly with nature.

Other tool-related things that are especially important to me are

PEOPLE

What role do other people play in your future work? How many do you want to interact with on a daily basis? What age group would you most enjoy working with? Pick as many as are true for you and feel free to add others.

	❑	I'd like to work with lots of people all day long.
	❑	I'd prefer to work alone most of the time.
	❑	I'd like to work as part of a team.
	❑	I'd like to work with people I might choose as friends.
	❑	I'd like to work with babies, children, or teenagers,
	❑	I'd like to work mostly with elderly people.
	❑	I'd like to work mostly with people who are in trouble.
	❑	I'd like to work mostly with people who are ill.

Other people-related things that are especially important to me are

PREPARATION

When you think about your future work, how much time and energy do you want to devote to preparing for it? Pick as many as are true for you and feel free to add others.

	❏	I want to find a job that requires a college degree.
	❏	I want to find a job where I could learn what I need to know on the job.
	❏	I want to find a job that requires no additional training after I graduate from high school.
	❏	I want to find a job where the more education I get, the better my chances for a better job.
	❏	I want to run my own business and be my own boss.

Other preparation-related things that are especially important to me are

Now that you've uncovered some word clues about the types of values that are most important to you, use the grid on the following page (or use a separate sheet of paper if this book does not belong to you) to "paint a picture" of your ideal future career. Use the icons as ideas for how to visualize each statement. Or, if you'd like to get really creative, get a large sheet of paper, some markers, magazines, and glue or tape and create a collage.

PURPOSE	PLACE	TIME
TOOLS	**PEOPLE**	**PREPARATION**

DISCOVER #3: DANGEROUS DETOURS

Half of figuring out what you do want to do is figuring out what you don't want to do. Get a jump start on this process by making a list of 10 careers you already know you absolutely don't want to do.

Warning: Failure to heed early warnings signs to avoid careers like this can result in long hours of boredom and frustration spent doing a job you just weren't meant to do.

(If this book does not belong to you, make your list on a separate sheet of paper.)

1. _____   _____
2. _____   _____
3. _____   _____

4. _____   _____

5. _____   _____

6. _____   _____

7. _____   _____

8. _____   _____

9. _____   _____

10. _____   _____

Red Flag Summary:
Look over your list, and in the second column above (or on a separate sheet of paper) see if you can summarize what it is about these jobs that makes you want to avoid them like a bad case of cooties.

DISCOVER #4: ULTIMATE CAREER DESTINATION

Imagine that your dream job is like a favorite tourist destination, and you have to convince other people to pick it over every other career in the world. How would you describe it? What features make it especially appealing to you? What does a person have to do to have a career like it?

Take a blank sheet of paper and fold it into thirds. Fill each column on both sides with words and pictures that create a vivid image of what you'd most like your future career to be.

Special note: Just for now, instead of actually naming a specific career, describe what your ideal career would be like. In places where the name of the career would be used, leave a blank space like this _____. For instance: For people who want to become rich and famous, being a _____ is the way to go.

GET IN GEAR!

YOU ARE HERE

DISCOVER #5: GET SOME DIRECTION

It's easy to get lost when you don't have a good idea of where you want to go. This is especially true when you start thinking about what to do with the rest of your life. Unless you focus on where you want to go, you might get lost or even miss the exit. This discover exercise will help you connect your own interests and abilities with a whole world of career opportunities.

Mark the activities that you enjoy doing or would enjoy doing if you had the chance. Be picky. Don't mark ideas that you wish you would do. Mark only those that you would really do. For instance, if skydiving sounds appealing but you'd never do it because you are terrified of heights, don't mark it.

Please Note: If this book does not belong to you, write your responses on a separate sheet of paper.

❑ 1. Rescue a cat stuck in a tree
❑ 2. Visit the pet store every time you go to the mall
❑ 3. Paint a mural on the cafeteria wall
❑ 4. Send e-mail to a "pen pal" in another state
❑ 5. Survey your classmates to find out what they do after school
❑ 6. Run for student council
❑ 7. Try out for the school play
❑ 8. Dissect a frog and identify the different organs
❑ 9. Play baseball, soccer, football, or _____ (fill in your favorite sport)

❏ 10. Talk on the phone to just about anyone who will talk back
❏ 11. Try foods from all over the world—Thailand, Poland, Japan, etc.
❏ 12. Write poems about things happening in your life
❏ 13. Create a really scary haunted house to take your friends through on Halloween
❏ 14. Recycle all your family's trash
❏ 15. Bake a cake and decorate it for your best friend's birthday
❏ 16. Simulate an imaginary flight through space on your computer screen
❏ 17. Build model airplanes, boats, dollhouses, or anything from kits
❏ 18. Sell enough advertisements for the school yearbook to win a trip to Walt Disney World
❏ 19. Teach your friends a new dance routine
❏ 20. Watch the stars come out at night and see how many constellations you can find
❏ 21. Watch baseball, soccer, football, or _____ (fill in your favorite sport) on TV
❏ 22. Give a speech in front of the entire school
❏ 23. Plan the class field trip to Washington, D.C.
❏ 24. Read everything in sight, including the back of the cereal box
❏ 25. Figure out "who dunnit" in a mystery story
❏ 26. Take in stray or hurt animals
❏ 27. Make a poster announcing the school football game
❏ 28. Put together a multimedia show for a school assembly using music and lots of pictures and graphics
❏ 29. Think up a new way to make the lunch line move faster and explain it to the cafeteria staff
❏ 30. Invest your allowance in the stock market and keep track of how it does
❏ 31. Go to the ballet or opera every time you get the chance
❏ 32. Do experiments with a chemistry set
❏ 33. Keep score at your sister's Little League game
❏ 34. Use lots of funny voices when reading stories to children

□ 35. Ride airplanes, trains, boats—anything that moves

□ 36. Interview the new exchange student for an article in the school newspaper

□ 37. Build your own treehouse

□ 38. Help clean up a waste site in your neighborhood

□ 39. Visit an art museum and pick out your favorite painting

□ 40. Make a chart on the computer to show how much soda students buy from the school vending machines each week

□ 41. Keep track of how much your team earns to buy new uniforms

□ 42. Play Monopoly in an all-night championship challenge

□ 43. Play an instrument in the school band or orchestra

□ 44. Take things apart and put them back together again

□ 45. Write stories about sports for the school newspaper

□ 46. Listen to other people talk about their problems

□ 47. Imagine yourself in exotic places

□ 48. Hang around bookstores and libraries

❏ 49. Play harmless practical jokes on April Fools' Day
❏ 50. Join the 4-H club at your school
❏ 51. Take photographs at the school talent show
❏ 52. Create an imaginary city using a computer
❏ 53. Do 3-D puzzles
❏ 54. Make money by setting up your own business—
paper route, lemonade stand, etc.
❏ 55. Keep track of the top 10 songs of the week
❏ 56. Read about famous inventors and their inventions
❏ 57. Make play-by-play announcements at the school
football game
❏ 58. Answer phones during a telethon to raise money
for orphans
❏ 59. Be an exchange student in another country
❏ 60. Write down all your secret thoughts and favorite
sayings in a journal
❏ 61. Jump out of an airplane (with a parachute, of course)
❏ 62. Plant and grow a garden in your backyard (or
on your windowsill)
❏ 63. Use a video camera to make your own movies

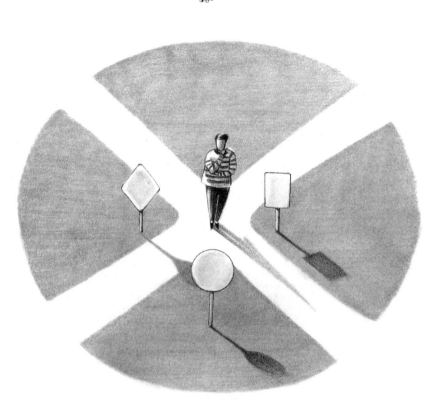

❏ 64. Get your friends together to help clean up your town after a hurricane or other natural disaster

❏ 65. Spend your summer at a computer camp learning lots of new computer programs

❏ 66. Build bridges, skyscrapers, and other structures out of LEGOs

❏ 67. Plan a concert in the park for little kids

❏ 68. Collect different kinds of rocks

❏ 69. Help plan a sports tournament

❏ 70. Be DJ for the school dance

❏ 71. Learn how to fly a plane or sail a boat

❏ 72. Write funny captions for pictures in the school yearbook

❏ 73. Scuba dive to search for buried treasure

❏ 74. Recognize and name several different breeds of cats, dogs, and other animals

❏ 75. Sketch pictures of your friends

❏ 76. Pick out neat stuff to sell at the school store
❏ 77. Answer your classmates' questions about how to use the computer
❏ 78. Draw a map showing how to get to your house from school
❏ 79. Make up new words to your favorite songs
❏ 80. Take a hike and name the different kinds of trees, birds, or flowers
❏ 81. Referee intramural basketball games
❏ 82. Join the school debate team
❏ 83. Make a poster with postcards from all the places you went on your summer vacation
❏ 84. Write down stories that your grandparents tell you about when they were young

CALCULATE THE CLUES

Now is your chance to add it all up. Each of the 12 boxes on the following pages contains an interest area that is common to both your world and the world of work. Follow these directions to discover your personal Skill Set:

1. Find all of the numbers that you checked on pages 18–23 in the following boxes and mark

them with an X. Work your way all the way through number 84.

2. Go back and count the Xs marked for each interest area. Write that number in the space that says "Total."
3. Find the interest area with the highest total and put a number one in the "Rank" blank of that box. Repeat this process for the next two highest scoring areas. Rank the second highest as number two and the third highest as number three.
4. If you have more than three strong areas, choose the three that are most important and interesting to you.

Remember: If this book does not belong to you, write your responses on a separate sheet of paper.

ADVENTURE

❑ 1
❑ 13
❑ 25
❑ 37
❑ 49
❑ 61
❑ 73
Total: _____
Rank: _____

ANIMALS & NATURE

❑ 2
❑ 14
❑ 26
❑ 38
❑ 50
❑ 62
❑ 74
Total: _____
Rank: _____

ART

❑ 3
❑ 15
❑ 27
❑ 39
❑ 51
❑ 63
❑ 75
Total: _____
Rank: _____

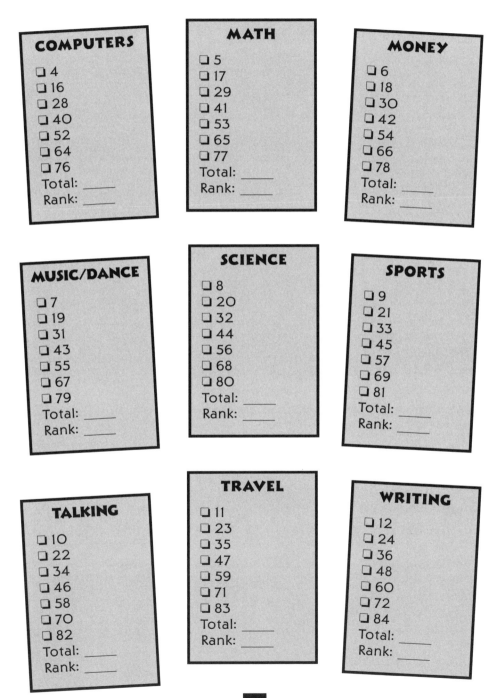

COMPUTERS

- ❏ 4
- ❏ 16
- ❏ 28
- ❏ 40
- ❏ 52
- ❏ 64
- ❏ 76

Total: _____

Rank: _____

MATH

- ❏ 5
- ❏ 17
- ❏ 29
- ❏ 41
- ❏ 53
- ❏ 65
- ❏ 77

Total: _____

Rank: _____

MONEY

- ❏ 6
- ❏ 18
- ❏ 30
- ❏ 42
- ❏ 54
- ❏ 66
- ❏ 78

Total: _____

Rank: _____

MUSIC/DANCE

- ❏ 7
- ❏ 19
- ❏ 31
- ❏ 43
- ❏ 55
- ❏ 67
- ❏ 79

Total: _____

Rank: _____

SCIENCE

- ❏ 8
- ❏ 20
- ❏ 32
- ❏ 44
- ❏ 56
- ❏ 68
- ❏ 80

Total: _____

Rank: _____

SPORTS

- ❏ 9
- ❏ 21
- ❏ 33
- ❏ 45
- ❏ 57
- ❏ 69
- ❏ 81

Total: _____

Rank: _____

TALKING

- ❏ 10
- ❏ 22
- ❏ 34
- ❏ 46
- ❏ 58
- ❏ 70
- ❏ 82

Total: _____

Rank: _____

TRAVEL

- ❏ 11
- ❏ 23
- ❏ 35
- ❏ 47
- ❏ 59
- ❏ 71
- ❏ 83

Total: _____

Rank: _____

WRITING

- ❏ 12
- ❏ 24
- ❏ 36
- ❏ 48
- ❏ 60
- ❏ 72
- ❏ 84

Total: _____

Rank: _____

What are your top three interest areas? List them here (or on a separate piece of paper).

1. _____

2. _____

3. _____

This is your personal Skill Set and provides important clues about the kinds of work you're most likely to enjoy. Remember it and look for career ideas with a Skill Set that matches yours most closely. You'll find a Skill Set box at the beginning of each career profile in the following section.

TAKE A TRIP!

Cruise down the
career idea highway
and enjoy in-depth profiles of some of the interesting
options in this field. Keep in mind all that you've discovered
about yourself so far. Find the careers that match your own
Skill Set first. After that, keep on trucking through the other
ideas—exploration is the name of this game.

Math and money. Add these two ingredients to a career
search and you're bound to find quite a number of career
ideas that equal success. Whether your focus is on the bottom line or on complex equations, math and money skills can
provide the means for making a good living while remaining
true to yourself and all that you have to offer the world.

On one hand, if you can find a way to mix earning money
with doing something that you really like to do, you'll have
it made. When you look at people who have done this in a
big way, you tend to see a couple of factors at play. Either
they are doing something that involves lots of skill and

expertise that other people will pay lots of money to get, or they are doing something in an innovative way that creates new opportunity.

On the other hand, math is the cornerstone of some very exciting career choices too. You may already associate math with careers like banking and accounting but other possibilities may surprise you. In fact, math is a common denominator in a wide variety of interesting and well-paying jobs. Math skills are in such high demand that math-intensive jobs like actuary, software engineer, computer analyst, mathematician, and statistician put in frequent appearances on "best jobs" lists.

As you read about the following careers, imagine yourself doing each job and ask yourself the following questions:

- Would I like it?
- Would I be good at it?
- Is it the stuff my career dreams are made of?

If so, make a quick exit to explore what it involves, try it out, check it out, and get acquainted! Look out for the symbols below.

Buckle up and enjoy the trip!

☞ TRY IT OUT

✔ CHECK IT OUT

🖱 ON THE WEB

📚 AT THE LIBRARY

🗣 WITH THE EXPERTS

A NOTE ON WEB SITES
Internet sites tend to move around the Web a bit. If you have trouble finding a particular site, use an Internet browser to find a specific Web site or type of information.

Actuary

SKILL SET

✔ MATH

✔ COMPUTERS

✔ TALKING

WHAT IS AN ACTUARY?

Go ahead, admit it. You don't have a clue about what an actuary actually does, do you? That's OK. Even some adults aren't familiar with this career, although whether they know it or not, most people are affected in some way by the work actuaries do.

The job title actuary makes regular appearances on several "best careers" and "top careers" lists. It routinely makes top 10 and every once in a while shows up in the number-one spot in lists that rank the best jobs in America. These listings rank jobs according to work environment, salary, availability of jobs, job security, and stress levels. Obviously, the career consistently ranks high in each of these areas in order to retain its winning streak.

According to the Society of Actuaries, actuaries are professionals who are trained in mathematics, statistics, and economic techniques that allow them to put a financial value on future events. It's like putting a price tag on future risks. These risks might include hazards ranging from a natural disaster and its potential impact on a community or industry, to the chances that an average 45-year-old, nonsmoking, overweight male has of suffering a heart attack.

One way to describe what actuaries do is to think of them as financial architects or social mathematicians. They use a unique combination of analytical and business skills to help solve any number of business-related or people-related problems.

In addition to having top-notch math skills, successful actuaries must also be well informed on matters relating to business issues and trends, social science, law, and economics. They must be team players who are comfortable working with all kinds of people, and they must be good communicators—especially when it comes to explaining the complex work they do in simple terms that others can understand. Perhaps the most important skill is problem solving. Actuaries have to like solving problems and to be good at it too.

At least half of all actuaries practicing in the United States work in the insurance industry where their main function is to figure out how much insurance companies should charge for specific types of insurance policies. Other actuaries work in government, helping to manage programs such as Social Security and Medicare. Banks, investment firms, large corporations, accounting firms, and labor unions are other places where actuaries work.

To prepare for a career as an actuary, you will need a college degree. Some actuaries actually major in math or actuarial science, while others major in subjects such as economics, liberal arts, or finance. Whichever route you take, it pays

to get a well-rounded education and to pick up good study habits.

In order to achieve professional status, actuaries earn the coveted title of "fellow" in one of the professional societies. To get the best jobs, actuaries must pass a series of tough examinations. Many actuaries start preparing for and taking the initial exams while they are still in college. These exams test basic mathematical skills in areas such as probability, calculus, and algebra and they are good indications of your aptitude with numbers. Subsequent exams cover topics such as finance, economics, accounting, and insurance law. Experts recommend that actuaries get a few years of experience before tackling these types of exams. Ten years is not an unusual time span for someone to complete all of the exams. Fortunately, once you have landed a job as an actuary, most employers will allow you to use some of your work time to study for the exams, so you get to earn while you learn.

☞ TRY IT OUT

BE AN ACTUARY

Find all kinds of useful information about what it's like to be an actuary at the Be an Actuary Web site at http://www. beanactuary.org. While you're there be sure to take the "skills quiz" and find out if your skills and interests match those required to succeed in this profession.

Once you've explored enough to qualify as something of an actuarial expert, use your newfound knowledge to create a poster or brochure that will help other kids understand what an actuary does.

 CHECK IT OUT

🖱 ON THE WEB
KNOW YOUR NUMBERS

Having a way with numbers is key to the success of an actuary. You can get a head start and have a lot of fun in the process by visiting this interactive Web site: http://www. cut-the-knot.com. Here you'll find games and puzzles, an inventor's paradox, and lots more. Make sure to give the probability activities a whirl. It will be great practice for your work as an actuary.

Then, sharpen your problem-solving (and puzzle-making!) skills at the Discovery School's Puzzlemaker Web site at http:// puzzlemaker.school.discovery.com.

FUNERCISE FOR THE BRAIN
Flex your mental muscles and have some fun at some of these math Web sites just for kids:

- A+ Math at http://www.aplusmath.com/games
- Brainbashers at http://www.brainbashers.com
- Cool Math 4 Kids at http://www.coolmath4kids.com
- Figure This! at http://www.figurethis.org
- Math Arcade at http://www.funbrain.com

AT THE LIBRARY
DO YOU SUDOKU?
Join the crowd and get hooked on Sudoku, a Japanese number game that's lots of fun. Warning: This game can be addictive!

Chisholm, Alastair. *The Kid's Book of Sudoku 1*. New York: Simon and Schuster, 2005.
Puzzler Media. *Original Sudoku for Kids*. New York: Thunder's Mouth, 2005.
Small, Lindsay. *Superstar Sudoku for Kids*. New York: Price Stern Sloan, 2005.

Or go online for instructions and opportunities to play at http://www.soduku.org.

MATH IS MURDER
What do solving mysteries and solving math problems have in common? It takes logic to solve them both. And, since

thinking logically is one of the things that actuaries do best, here's your chance to jump-start your logic skills (and have a little fun while you're at it). Get started with these books:

Cameron, Vicki. *Clue Mysteries: 15 Whodunits to Solve in Minutes.* Philadelphia: Running, 2003.
Weber, Ken. *Five Minute Mysteries.* Philadelphia: Running Press, 2005.
———. *Utterly Ingenious Five-Minute Mysteries.* Philadelphia: Running Press Press, 2003.

🗣 WITH THE EXPERTS

American Academy of Actuaries
1100 17th Street NW, 7th Floor
Washington, DC 20036-4601
http://www.actuary.org

American Society of Pension Professionals & Actuaries
4245 North Fairfax Drive, Suite 750
Arlington, VA 22203-1637
http://www.aspa.org

Casualty Actuarial Society
4350 North Fairfax Drive, Suite 250
Arlington, VA 22203-1695
http://www.casact.org

International Association of Black Actuaries
1115 Inman Avenue, Suite 235
Edison, NJ 08820-1132
http://www.blackactuaries.org

Society of Actuaries
475 North Martingale, #600
Schaumburg, IL 60173-2405
http://www.soa.org

GET ACQUAINTED

Sharon Robinson, Actuary

CAREER PATH

CHILDHOOD ASPIRATION: To be an interior designer or an engineer like her big brother.

FIRST JOB: Cashier at a pharmacy.

CURRENT JOB: Vice president and pricing actuary for medical professional liability for a major property casualty insurance company.

A GOOD GUESS

Sharon Robinson admits that the way she chose her career wasn't exactly scientific. When she was in high school, she read an article called something like "101 Careers You Should Know About." The article listed several math-related careers and gave addresses for more information. Robinson sent letters to some of the organizations mentioned in the article. The only response she got was from the Society of Actuaries, which sent her a packet full of interesting information. She thought the career sounded pretty good, so she decided to become an actuary. It's not a method that would work for everyone, but fortunately, it's worked very well for Robinson.

HARDER THAN IT LOOKED

From the very first day of college, Robinson declared her major as actuarial science. The more courses she took, the more she enjoyed it, so she knew she'd made the right choice. She quickly learned that in order to be certified, actuaries have to pass a series of exams. She was doing so well in her courses that she decided to get a head start on the process and sat for the first exam during her first year of college.

Big mistake! It was a disaster. Robinson flunked the exam—badly. Not having had any experience in flunking exams, she was devastated. It took her three tries to pass the first exam, and along the way she learned an important lesson. This was no ordinary exam. By the third round, she had fine-tuned her study process so that she started studying every day—months in advance. She faithfully kept a log of the hours she spent preparing and discovered that 400 hours of study did the trick. That's what it took to pass each exam.

Those exams were the toughest part of the entire process, but Robinson hung in there to pass them and eventually earned the coveted designation of fellow in the Casualty Actuarial Society. The hard work proved worthwhile, because once she completed the exams, she was rewarded with a major job promotion. Even now, her skills and her certification continue to be in high demand.

A GOOD DAY'S WORK

Robinson is the pricing actuary in charge of her company's medical professional liability business segment. The company insures a wide variety of health care providers such as hospitals, physicians and surgeons, dentists, and nursing homes. As you can probably imagine, the potential for liability claims varies quite a bit depending on what kind of care and treatment the client provides, the practices in place to avoid and control medical errors, and even the legal environment in the location where the client works. For example, the cost of insuring a dentist who performs oral surgery would be different from the cost for one who only handles routine dental care. It's Robinson's job to put a price tag on the risks associated with these factors and many more.

As vice president, Robinson also manages a staff of 12 actuarial professionals who support the pricing work for the business unit. So her work these days involves just as much project management, coaching, and counseling as it does pricing analysis. She often uses a computer to organize data and develop statistical models that help guide their decisions.

With people's lives, health, and businesses at stake, Robinson and her team work especially hard to get things right so clients have adequate protection.

A CRYSTAL BALL

Along with determining appropriate pricing for all of the different types of health care facilities and providers the company insures, another part of Robinson's job is looking ahead. She reports to the senior vice president responsible for the health care industry segment; she advises him about trends in the industry and helps guide the department's long-term business strategies. Some of this involves analyzing the potential impact of unknown events such as changes in the legal environment governing medical malpractice or changes in technology affecting the practice of medicine.

A SATISFYING CAREER

While Robinson enjoys the mathematical challenges of the job, she is quick to point out that it's not just number crunching. The job is very people-oriented and requires her to interface with all kinds, including underwriters, claim handlers, attorneys, and senior managers. She says technical skills alone won't cut it in this work. Good communication skills are key to success as an actuary.

As Robinson has progressed through her career, she's learned what she likes most about the actuary field. Her profession has a very well-defined career track, it is well respected in the insurance industry, and there is an excellent job market.

Sounds like she'd agree with those top career lists!

Advertising Executive

SHORTCUTS

SKILL SET

✔ ART

✔ WRITING

✔ MONEY

GO walk around town and see how many different kinds of advertising you spot—billboards, signs, posters, etc.

READ the ads in different kinds of magazines and see if you can tell what kinds of buyers they are trying to reach.

TRY making a list of your all-time favorite television commercials. If you noticed them and remember them, they are doing what they are supposed to do.

WHAT IS AN ADVERTISING EXECUTIVE?

Just do it. Have it your way. When you care enough to send the very best. If you know that those slogans belong to Nike, Burger King, and Hallmark, it's because an advertising executive has done his or her job well. Companies like these spend more than $100 billion each year to get their names recognized and their products bought.

Advertising executives are the professionals they depend on to get the job done. Advertising executives generally possess a unique combination of artistic creativity and business savvy. They take the lead on advertising campaigns and projects. Sometimes ad execs may work primarily for one big client. Other times they work on a variety of smaller accounts. In either case the client is investing lots of money—sometimes millions of dollars—for advertising, and they expect a big return in increased name recognition and sales. Clients depend on advertising executives to deliver fresh, effective ideas in a professional, businesslike way.

Advertising executives spend their days schmoozing with clients, brainstorming ideas with other project team members, reviewing demographic research, and handling any of the zillions of details associated with an advertising campaign. The pace can be fast and intense.

New York and Chicago are considered two of the hot spots for advertising, and many of the major clients do business with big advertising firms with headquarters in these places. However, with increases in international advertising, you are just as likely to find branch offices in Bangkok, Thailand, as you are in Los Angeles, California. Along with the big firms, there are also growing numbers of smaller, and yes, entrepreneurial firms found just about anywhere. Although the common wisdom has these small firms handling more local accounts, they sometimes beat the big guys to the punch by presenting unique ideas and highly customized services to national clients.

Like any job, advertising has its pros and cons. On the plus side is the chance to let your creative juices flow. Advertising can be fun work, and seeing your work on TV, in magazines, and on billboards can be a real kick. There's lots of variety and plenty of challenge to keep things from getting boring too.

On the downside is the continual need to please clients. Sometimes the client's idea of good advertising doesn't jibe with yours, but guess who wins? You got it. The client is always right and you better not forget it. There can also be a lot of stress associated with advertising because of tight deadlines.

The hours can be long and the competition tough. But it can all be worth it when things come together and everybody starts noticing your work.

Other types of jobs found in the advertising agency include the following:

Account managers work as liaisons between the client and the advertising agency and make sure that everyone is working toward the same goals.

Copywriters, art directors, and **creative directors** are the people found in the creative departments of ad agencies— where ads are written and designed.

Media buyers are the people who find out how much various media costs and make the arrangements to buy advertising space. They are the ones who figure out the best mix of television, radio, newspaper, magazine, and other media for a specific advertising campaign. These decisions are far from guesswork. Instead they are based on lots of research.

Production managers oversee the actual production of an advertising piece whether it is for radio, television, or some sort of print medium like a newspaper or magazine.

While it almost always takes a degree in advertising, marketing, or some other business-related field to get your foot in the door at an advertising agency, there is only one thing that will keep you there: talent. An advertising executive is only as good as his or her last successful project. Creativity, fresh and innovative ideas, a way with words, and some artistic flair are what it takes to thrive in this exciting profession.

 **TRY IT OUT**

GET YOUR BOOK TOGETHER
Something that all advertising professionals have in common is a portfolio, affectionately known as a "book." Depending on where someone is in his or her career, this book may contain

either storyboards from actual advertising campaigns he or she has worked on or, if the person is new to the game, storyboards from advertising campaigns he or she would have liked to work on. One of the best ways for you to find out if you'd like to make your career in advertising is to put your own book together.

All you need is a product, some great ideas, and a way to illustrate your ideas. First, pick a product that you really like—maybe a soft drink or a certain brand of sneakers. Next, think of the type of person most likely to buy that product and jot down ideas that might entice your audience to buy the product. Keep those ideas coming!

Finally, use markers, pictures cut from magazines, or computer graphics to put together your own ads. Try coming up with several different approaches for each product. Repeat this process several times and you'll have your first advertising "book" made up of fictitious campaigns for real products.

✔ CHECK IT OUT

🖱 ON THE WEB

HOT OFF THE PRESS

For the absolutely latest news in advertising visit Adweek Online at http://www.adweek.com. It's the place ad execs go to find out who's who and what's what in advertising. Be sure to look at the Best Spots pages. That's where the professionals spotlight the best new ads.

ADVERTISER FOR HIRE

If you really want to know what kinds of opportunities are out there, fast-forward your life about 10 years and pretend that you are a recent college graduate looking for a lucky break in advertising. You won a college advertising competition and worked as an intern for an ad agency for two summers.

With that scenario in mind, see what kinds of jobs you'd qualify for at Monster.com (http://www.monster.com). Under job category, scroll down to "Advertising/Marketing/Public

Relations"; then select a job location where you'd someday like to work.

Use the information you find there to write a description of your dream job in advertising.

ADVERTISING 101

Want a quick lesson in how the advertising game is played? Look at the Web sites of some of America's top advertising agencies and see how they advertise themselves. First, make a list of the following companies and rate their performance. Make sure to jot down a few notes about why you do (or don't) like their approach. Here are Web sites for the some of the biggest and best ad firms:

- J. Walter Thompson at http://www.jwt.com
- Leo Burnett at http://www.leoburnett.com
- Ogilvy & Mather at http://www.ogilvy.com
- Saatchi & Saatchi at http://www.saatchi-saatchi.com
- Young & Rubicam at http://www.yr.com

AND THE WINNER IS . . .

Movies have the Oscars, music has the Grammys, and advertising has the Clio Awards. It's a BIG deal to win a Clio. Take a look at the latest winners and see what you think of them. Are they really the cream of the crop or just overdone flops? Catch all the excitement at http://www.clioawards.com.

AT THE LIBRARY
THE WORD ON ADVERTISING

Speaking of books, here are some books that provide more information about careers in advertising and public relations:

Field, Shelley. *Career Opportunities in Advertising and Public Relations, Fourth Edition.* New York: Ferguson, 2006.
Ferguson. *Discovering Careers For Your Future: Advertising and Marketing.* New York: Ferguson, 2005.

Wetfeet. *Careers in Advertising and Public Relations: A Wet-Feet Guide.* San Francisco: WetFeet, 2004.

To find out more about advertising's role in the media and as a social force, read:

Egendorf, Laura. *Advertising: Opposing Viewpoints.* Farmington Hills, Mich.: Greenhaven, 2005.

Gifford, Clive. *Advertising and Marketing: Influences and Persuasion.* Portsmouth, N.H.: Heinemann, 2005.

Graydon, Shar. *Made You Look: How Advertising Works and Why You Should Know.* Plattsburgh, N.Y.: Tundra Books, 2003.

Petley, Julian. *Advertising: Media Wise.* North Mankato, Minn.: Smart Apple Media, 2004.

🗣 WITH THE EXPERTS

The Ad Council
261 Madison Avenue, 11th Floor
New York, NY 10016-2303
http://www.adcouncil.com

American Advertising Federation
1101 Vermont Avenue NW, Suite 500
Washington, DC 20005-6306
http://www.aaf.org

American Association of Advertising Agencies
405 Lexington Avenue, 18th Floor
New York, NY 10174-1801
http://www.aaaa.org

American Marketing Association
311 South Wacker Drive, Suite 5800
Chicago, IL 60606-6627
http://www.marketingpower.com

Association of National Advertisers
708 Third Avenue
New York, NY 10017-4270
http://www.ana.net

International Advertising Association
521 Fifth Avenue, Suite 1807
New York, NY 10175-0003
http://www.iaaglobal.org

Public Relations Society of America
33 Maiden Lane, 11th Floor
New York, NY 10038-5150
http://www.prsa.org

GET ACQUAINTED

Whit Friese,
Advertising Executive

CAREER PATH

CHILDHOOD ASPIRATION:
To be a professional football player.

FIRST JOB: Working at a miniature golf course.

CURRENT JOB: Executive Creative Director at the Tokyo office of Leo Burnett.

FATHER KNOWS BEST

Like a lot of young boys, Whit Friese wanted to play professional football when he grew up. The problem was that he didn't grow up quite big enough to make it as a pro. As a six-foot-tall and 165-pound high school junior, he started looking into other options. His dad happened to notice that Friese had a doodling habit; he drew goofy little drawings on everything he could get his hands on. Friese's dad must have thought the doodles were pretty good because one day he brought home for his son a book about careers in advertising.

The book got Friese interested enough to pursue a degree in advertising at Pennsylvania State University.

While in college, Friese took a lot of art classes that allowed him to cultivate his creative design skills. By the time he graduated from college, he was sure that he wanted to work on the creative side of advertising. He put his book together so he could show prospective employers what he could do with different kinds of products, headed back home to Chicago, and started hunting for a job.

A LUCKY BREAK . . . EVENTUALLY

Friese was a little disappointed that the advertising world didn't immediately welcome him with open arms. He took his book around to several big firms, but all had the same basic response: "Thanks, but no thanks." So Friese sold ads for a newspaper for about eight months until his job prospects took a definite turn for the better.

It wasn't just luck that turned things around. It was a winning combination of hard work and pure talent. Add just a dash of courage and you have the recipe for Friese's big splash into the advertising world. Instead of sitting around waiting for ad agencies to call, he looked for a way to get their attention. He entered an ad he designed in a national contest—and won. Several newspapers carried the story, and the story was seen by the powers that be at Leo Burnett, one of the biggest ad firms around. Someone realized they had Friese's book on file and gave him a call. As a result, he landed a plum position as an art director for the prestigious firm.

ADVERTISING AROUND THE WORLD

After showing some advertising muscle as creative director for the world's largest soft drink company in places as far flung as South Africa, Japan, India, and Europe, Friese was transferred to Leo Burnett's Tokyo, Japan, office (called Beacom Communications). As executive creative director, he co-runs a creative department of about 70 people—almost all Japanese. His department works on multinational accounts including McDonalds, Proctor & Gamble, and Philip Morris, as well as many domestic brands.

Friese says that the move to Japan has been like starting over. He's found that the Japanese market is a very unique place where what you say and how you say it is very different from the United States. And he doesn't mean the language. See for yourself what he's talking about at the company's Web site at http://www.beacomcom.co.jp.

A CONFESSION AND SOME ADVICE

Friese is the first to admit that he loves his job. He loves it so much, in fact, that it is not unusual for him to spend several hours at the office on Sunday just because he wants to be there.

He says that some of the best advice he's gotten came from his parents. They told him that if he really wanted to get into advertising, he could do it. They said that even if he had to take a few lumps along the way, it would be worth it. So far, they've been right.

Banker

SHORTCUTS

GO start a savings account at a nearby bank.

READ What Do Banks Do, by Roberta Basel (Makato, Minn.: Capstone Press, 2006).

TRY figuring out how much interest you could earn in a year by tucking away $500 in a savings account offering 5.25 percent annual interest.

WHAT IS A BANKER?

In case you haven't noticed, there's a lot of money floating around out there. Even kids like you have at least a little bit to spend—and when you put your little bit together with everyone else's little bits, that adds up to really big bucks. According to a study by Texas A&M University, in one year kids in the United States spend

- ☀ $2 billion on junk food
- ☀ $1.9 billion on toys and games
- ☀ $600 million on movies, shows, concerts, and sporting events
- ☀ $486 million on arcade video games
- ☀ $264 million on miscellaneous items such as stereos, cosmetics, and other living expenses

Now, if kids like you have that much money, just think of how much the adults with real jobs have! All that money is what keeps bankers in business. Bankers help people manage their money with savings accounts, checking accounts, credit cards, mortgage loans for houses, car loans, investment opportunities, and other types of financial services.

The banking industry as a whole offers many different kinds of career possibilities. Some specific options within the field include the following:

Commercial bankers work with businesses to handle their specialized banking needs.

Investment bankers manage investment portfolios for bank customers, including individuals, businesses, and governments.

Loan officers help customers in need of money to buy cars, consolidate debt, or make other major purchases.

Mortgage bankers work in the very specialized area of helping people secure loans for homes.

Trust officers handle special kinds of accounts called trusts, helps customers plan what to do with their money and assets after they die (called estate planning), and help customers manage inheritance income.

Opportunities in banks vary widely according to a person's education and experience. Someone with only a high school diploma might work as a teller, a customer service representative, a data entry clerk, or an administrative assistant. A college degree in finance, economics, accounting, or business broadens the range of opportunities to include commercial or consumer loan officer, bank manager, trust officer, investment banker, financial analyst, and other more specialized jobs. As is true of any profession, the highest salaries and best perks go to those who have the jobs with the highest levels of responsibility.

In addition to working at banks similar to those you see around your community, bankers may specialize in international banking, in securities firms (such as you'd find on Wall Street), and in government entities, such as the Department of the Treasury and the Federal Reserve Board.

Successful bankers know how to work with numbers and how to deal with people. They have a firm grasp of the role money plays in our world. If you think a career in banking might be a good choice for you, start getting ready now by taking classes in math, speech, and writing to develop your communication skills, and in business and economics to find out more about the world of money.

☞ TRY IT OUT

PRACTICE WHAT YOU PREACH
If you plan on making a career out of handling other people's money, first get a handle on your own. A basic rule of thumb in personal finance is this: For every dollar you earn, save or invest 10¢, give 10¢ away to a worthy cause, and spend the rest. To implement this plan, all you need is three containers with lids and a notebook. Label one container for each account: savings, charity, spending. Use the notebook to keep track of the cash flow (how the money is earned and what it's used for).

PLAY MONEY
Learn more about money by gathering a couple of friends for a go-for-broke round of either of these classic Milton Bradley board games: Monopoly or Life. Or go high-tech with either of these games in a computer format produced by Hasbro Interactive. Both games provide a fun way to learn your way around the world of money. Who ends up managing their money best?

✔ CHECK IT OUT

🖰 ON THE WEB
CYBERBANKING
You'll find all kinds of helpful information and really fun simulated banking activities on the Internet. Some sites to investigate are the following:

☼ Fed 101 at http://www.federalreserveeducation.org/
fed101/index.htm
☼ Kids Bank at http://www.kidsbank.com
☼ Young Investor at http://www.younginvestor.com

OUT-OF-THIS-WORLD BANKING

Two incredibly fun (and free) Internet games that will test
your banking skills include the following:

☼ Escape from Knab, at http://www.escapefromknab.
com, issues you a one-way ticket to the planet
Knab. Once you get there, you discover that a
return ticket costs $10,000. You have to get a job
to earn money and save enough to buy your way
back to Earth.
☼ Gazillionaire, at http://gazillionaire.com, is described
as a cross between Monopoly in outer space and Wall
Street in Wonderland. The game lets you head your
own trading company; it challenges you to sell 100
tons of cargo (moon fern or oggle sand, anyone?)
and earn 1 million "kubar" before your squid-faced
competition beats you to it.

AT THE LIBRARY
BOOKS YOU CAN BANK ON

A good banker is one who knows all about money—earning
it, spending it, and saving it. Start your own financial education with any of these entertaining and very informative
books.

Allman, Barbara. *Banking: How Economics Works.* Minneapolis:
Lerner, 2005.
Basel, Roberta. *Checks, Credits, and Debit Cards.* Mankato,
Minn.: Capstone, 2006.
———. *History of Money.* Mankato, Minn.: Capstone, 2006.
Godfrey, Neale S. *Neale S. Godfrey's Ultimate Kids Money
Book.* New York: Simon and Schuster, 1998.

Karlitz, Gail. *Growing Money: A Complete Investing Guide for Kids.* New York: Price Stern Sloan, 2001.

Macht, Norman L. *Money and Banking.* New York: Chelsea House, 2001.

McAlpine, Margaret. *Working in Banking and Finance.* Milwaukee, Wis.: Gareth Stevens, 2005.

WITH THE EXPERTS

American Bankers Association
1120 Conneticut Avenue NW
Washington, DC 20036-3902
http://www.aba.com

American Financial Services
  Association
919 18th Street NW, Suite 300
Washington, DC 20006-5503
http://www.americanfinsvcs.com

American League of Financial
  Institutions
900 19th Street NW, Suite 400
Washington, DC 20006-2105
http://www.alfi.org

Financial Women International
1027 West Roselawn Avenue
Roseville, MN 55113-6406
http://www.fwi.org

GET ACQUAINTED

B. LaRae Orullian, Banker

CAREER PATH

CHILDHOOD ASPIRATION: To be a math or gym teacher.

FIRST JOB: Picking strawberries for 5¢ a cup and cherries for 3¢ a pound when she was a young girl.

CURRENT JOB: Vice chair, board of directors, Guaranty Bank and board member of several other corporations.

A LONG WAY UP

LaRae Orullian began her climb to become the first female president of a bank from the bottom rung of the banking career ladder. Her first official title at a bank in Utah was messenger girl, and her duties ranged from delivering mail to running errands at the region's federal reserve bank. The work kept her out and about in the city, and she gave it her best. Her hard work was soon rewarded with a promotion to file clerk, and she started spending her days confined to the file room in the bank's vault. Then she was promoted to coin wrapper.

Make no mistake, however. In those days, there were no fancy machines to sort and count huge piles of coins. Instead, the coin wrappers had to master the technique of balancing a roll of coins in the palms of their hands while inserting them into paper wrappers. Orullian got pretty good at it!

Throughout all these early banking jobs, Orullian was also attending banking school at night. She'd recognized that a good education was key to getting the best banking jobs. She couldn't afford to quit her job and go to school full time, but she stuck with her schedule for 13 years until she earned three graduate certificates in banking. She went on to also earn a master's degree in real estate and mortgage banking.

FULL STEAM AHEAD

With a good education and lots of experience under her belt, Orullian left her hometown and headed off to make her mark on the banking world. Hoping to ultimately reach the U.S. financial center on Wall Street, she made what she assumed would be a temporary stop in Denver. There she was hired as a loan secretary, soon promoted to secretary to the president of a bank, and eventually promoted to executive vice president and director of the bank. The position made her the highest-ranking woman in Denver's banking community and one of very few women at that level in the entire country.

With a successful track record like that, it's easy to understand why some of her colleagues who were starting the Women's Bank asked her to become its first president—and she accepted. The whole idea of a women's bank was a bold departure from the way things were done back in the 1970s. Experts initially scoffed at the notion of running a bank that provided equal access to services and resources; however, the naysayers settled down when Orullian and the other 50 founders of the Women's Bank bucked tradition and sold $10 million in stock simply by telling their friends and business associates about the opportunity. Those who said it couldn't be done were silenced altogether the first day the Women's Bank opened and took in $1 million in deposits and $1 million a week for the next 12 weeks. The bank even made a profit in its first month—something that takes most banks a few years to achieve!

MORE THAN ONE WAY TO NEW YORK

Needless to say, Orullian's rise to become the first female president of a bank was widely regarded as a huge success. It also became apparent that Orullian didn't have to go all the way to Wall Street to meet her highest professional ambitions. Denver has kept her plenty busy as a banker.

Nevertheless, Orullian confesses that the New York dream never completely faded. To her surprise and pleasure, she found another way to get to New York.

Strangely enough, it all came about from a habit she'd developed as a teenager. Orullian has always been a tireless volunteer, and as an adult, her volunteer interests included raising funds for favorite charities and leadership positions with the Girl Scouts. All this work came together in a special way when Orullian was chosen to be president of Girl Scouts of the U.S.A. One of the perks of this volunteer position was her very own office at their national headquarters, located in New York City!

HANG IN THERE!

After all this time and all her accomplishments, Orullian still regards the advanced math courses she took in high school as some of the most important training she ever received. It was there, working on complex algebra equations, that she learned to stick with a problem until she found the solution. The mental discipline it takes to identify tough problems and work hard to solve them has served Orullian well—first as a student and now as a bank president, community volunteer, and corporate board chairperson.

Economist

SHORTCUTS

GO to the library and find out all you can about Adam Smith, the man many consider to be the father of economics, and John Maynard Keynes, one of the greatest economists of the 20th century.

READ the Wall Street Journal—everyday reading for any economist worth his or her salt.

TRY planning a budget of your personal expenses for a year, including food, clothes, entertainment, and other must-have items.

SKILL SET

✔ MATH
✔ BUSINESS
✔ COMPUTERS

WHAT IS AN ECONOMIST?

An economist is a social scientist who solves the mysteries of how people and society operate. An economist looks at why people do what they do, especially in terms of their resources, such as time, money, and material goods. An economist is guided by, and may even come up with, economic theories, such as supply and demand, and other more memorable nuggets of wisdom, such as "there's no such thing as a free lunch."

Some of the issues economists commonly deal with include international food supply, job opportunities, the banking system, health care services, urban community development, poverty, AIDS (acquired immunodeficiency syndrome) and other health concerns, corporate finance, international competition, and public utilities. But people with a strong background in economics are prepared to work in all kinds of professions, not just as an economist. Here are a few job titles you might aspire to: economic forecaster, international economist, investment banker, federal reserve bank officer, Bureau of Labor Statistics analyst, Federal Trade Commission commissioner, foreign service executive, business analyst, labor negotiator, and contract administrator.

To get started in an economics career, you'll need at least a bachelor's degree in economics. This major will focus on problem-solving skills and will require courses such as statistics, calculus, and computer science, which require strong math skills. It will also focus on economic principles based in history and social science. Economics can be a very challenging academic program, but it's one that is well regarded and that provides the winning ticket for a number of career choices.

An economics major in college could be a good choice for you if you are interested in a career in bank management, business, labor relations, operations analysis, or a management-level position in a government agency or corporation. Economists work in all aspects of business including manufacturing, mining, banking, insurance, and retailing. There are also opportunities in the sports, recreation, entertainment, and technology industries. And while economics provides many interesting career options in and of itself, it can also be used as a springboard to go into fields such as law, politics, and business.

Although there are no guarantees, evidence does support the idea that those employed in an economics-related profession tend to earn significantly more money than the national average. A survey conducted by the National Association of Business Economists found that the average salary for business economists was $70,000.

☞ TRY IT OUT

TOYS FOR EVERYONE

If you are interested in a career in business economics, the following activity will give you an idea of the type of work you might do. Pretend that you are president of an international toy company. Your latest gizmo is selling so well in the United States that you want to expand into other countries' markets. Pick a country where you want to start and answer the following questions:

- ☼ Where is the country?
- ☼ How large is it (in population, national income, and geographic size) compared to the United States?
- ☼ How many children under the age of 12 live there?
- ☼ How much money do most of the adults earn each year?

To find answers to your questions, use the CIA's World Factbook, which can be consulted online at

- ☼ http://www.cia.gov/cia/publications/factbook
- ☼ http://www.countryreports.org

You may want to ask a parent or teacher to help you find these answers. Once you have, write up a brief report with your recommendation of whether or not the country would be a good market for your toys.

ECONOMIC DETECTIVE

Travel the world while tracking down the infamous and elusive Gang of 15 at this fun Web site: http://ecedweb.unomaha.edu/gang1.htm. While you're solving the mystery, you'll learn about the currencies of other countries and exchange rates and get a taste of international economics. Make a chart with 15 columns to record what you discover about each of the gang's destinations.

✔ CHECK IT OUT

🖱 ON THE WEB

ECONOMIC FUN AND GAMES

If you feel a little intimidated about the idea of an economics career, there are a few Web sites that will let you wade your way into some important economic principles and have a little fun at the same time.

- ☿ First, try out Ken White's Coin Flipping Page (http://shazam.econ.ubc.ca/flip). Here you can test your skills in probability and statistics.
- ☿ Peanuts or crackerjacks? Decide for yourself at the Federal Reserve Bank of Boston's fun educational Web site featuring the economics of pro sports at http://www.bos.frb.org/peanuts/leadpgs/intro.htm.
- ☿ Learn all about the "history in your pocket" at the U.S. Mint's h.i.p. Web site at http://www.usmint.gov/kids/flashIndex.cfm.
- ☿ Find links to a bunch of kid-friendly Web sites about economics at http://www.kathimitchell.com/econ.htm.

Now, if you are ready to jump in with both feet, go to the National Budget Simulation game at http://www.budgetsim.org/nbs where you'll have a chance to balance the national budget. Start with the short version of the game to learn the basics. Once you get the hang of it, move on to the long version where you'll get into some of the nitty-gritty details of economics.

ECONOMIC TREASURE HUNT

For a treasure chest full of fun (and dare we admit it?) educational activities, visit the Federal Reserve Bank of San Francisco Web site at http://www.frbsf.org/education/activities/index.html. There you'll get a chance to visit Fedville, play the Fed Chairman game, and go on a treasure hunt with some of the world's greatest economists.

GLOBAL GROCERIES

Join students from other countries on a global grocery shopping spree at http://www.landmark-project.com/ggl.index. html. Pick a favorite food and compare prices with students from all over the world. This Landmark Project Web site has been active since 1987, so there is plenty of information for you to compute, analyze, and discuss—just like a real international economist!

AT THE LIBRARY
THE WELL-READ ECONOMIST

If books are your preferred method of learning, here's a list to begin your economic education:

Donovan, Sandra. *Budgeting: How Economics Works*. Minneapolis: Lerner, 2005.

Gilman, Laura Anne. *Economics: How Economics Work*. Minneapolis: Lerner, 2005.

Kiyosaki, Robert, and Sharon Lechter. *Rich Dad's Escape from the Rat Race: How to Become a Rich Kid Following Rich Dad's Advice*. Boston: Little Brown, 2005.

Lewin, Ted. *How Much? Visiting Markets Around the World*. New York: Harper Collins, 2006.

Ranic, Bill. *Beyond the Lemonade Stand*. New York: Razorbill, 2005.

Teichmann, Iris. *Globalization*. North Mankato, Minn.: Smart Apple Media, 2003.

Welch, Deborah. *Economic Issues and Development: Contemporary Native American Issues*. New York: Chelsea House, 2005.

WITH THE EXPERTS

American Economic Association
2014 Broadway, Suite 305
Nashville, TN 37203-2407
http://www.vanderbilt.edu/AEA/org.htm

National Association for Business Economics
1233 20th Street NW, Suite 505
Washington, DC 20036-2304
http://www.nabe.com

National Council on Economic Education
1140 Avenue of the Americas
New York, NY 10036-5803
http://www.ncee.net

National Economic Association
c/o Urban Institute
2100 M Street NW
Washington, DC 20037-1207
http://www.ncat.edu/neconasc

Western Economic Association International
7400 Center Avenue, Suite 109
Huntington Beach, CA 92647-3039
http://www.weainternational.org

GET ACQUAINTED

Henk-Jan Brinkman, Economist

CAREER PATH

CHILDHOOD ASPIRATION: To be a police officer.

FIRST JOB: Working for his neighbor's construction company.

CURRENT JOB: Economic affairs officer, United Nations.

HENK-JAN BRINKMAN

PLAN B

Henk-Jan Brinkman grew up in the Netherlands. By the time he got into high school, he was gearing up to follow in his father's footsteps as an engineer. That plan took an unexpected turn when he failed the final exam in high school and had to repeat his final year.

Given a year to reevaluate his career choice, Brinkman started asking his teachers for advice. One teacher suggested that if he wanted to make good money, he should study economics. Before long, Brinkman started looking into that profession. The more he found out about economics, the more he liked it. Like engineering, economics combined the study of math and science. But as a social science, it also added a human element. Brinkman found that at its very root, economics was all about improving the standard of living for people. This aspect appealed to Brinkman because he felt it would give him a chance to make a difference.

Looking back, Brinkman realizes how different his life would have been if he had passed that exam and become an engineer. He can honestly say, however, that he's very happy with the way things turned out.

A MAN WITHOUT A COUNTRY

After graduating from high school, Brinkman started his college education at the University of Groningen in the Netherlands. Doctoral economic studies brought him to the United States, where he studied at the New School for Social Research in New York and started working for the United Nations. He now works as a development economist specializing in Africa.

In order to work for the United Nations, Brinkman had to sign a contract promising that his allegiance would be to the world and not to any particular country. Even though the Netherlands is his homeland and the United States is where he is raising his own child, he has promised to work for the international common good.

ALL IN A DAY'S WORK

A typical day for Brinkman involves three types of activities. First, Brinkman spends some time reading newspapers, reports, and other resources and visiting Internet sites to find out what's happening in the world.

Second, Brinkman takes all the data and information that he acquires and analyzes what he's learned. Sometimes this means putting seemingly unrelated events together to determine their combined impact on a situation. For instance, the unusual El Niño weather patterns in 1997 and 1998 played an important role in economics around the world. Drought, hurricanes, and other weather-related catastrophes can have a major impact on entire nations. Studying and thinking through such issues allows economists like Brinkman to recognize and address problems and provide recommendations so that governments can make the most out of bad situations, especially before they happen.

Another part of this process might involve "what if" simulations. Brinkman has to imagine various situations and analyze how they would impact Africa. What if the stock market were to crash? What if there was a major oil embargo? What if the Asian nations were to suffer a major recession? What if prices of cocoa and coffee were to fall? Brinkman and his colleagues use a very powerful economic computer program called Project Link to help analyze these types of scenarios. This program is a huge model of the world economy that links individual countries to each other. It helps them determine the cause and effect of all kinds of global issues.

The third part of Brinkman's work involves writing reports. Every month, he must submit to the secretary general of the United Nations a report detailing the current happenings and any major economic developments in Africa. He's also responsible for writing about special issues such as developing nations that have debt they can't repay. A big project that Brinkman works on each year is the World Economic and Social Survey. This major report is used by the United Nations to identify and address international social and economic issues. To see samples of the kinds of reports Brinkman writes, visit the United Nation's Web site (http://www.un.org/esa).

ECONOMICS AND YOU

If you think a career in economics might be a good choice for you, Brinkman suggests you take classes in both math and social sciences. Read newspapers and know what's happening in other parts of the world. Curiosity is one of the best assets an economist can possess.

E-Merchant

SHORTCUTS

GO online and try your hand at creating a Web site. For ideas and instructions try Web Genies at http://www.webgenies.co.uk and Web Monkey at http://webmonkey.wired.com/webmonkey/kids.

READ about good Web page design by looking at bad Web page design at the Web Pages that Suck site at http://webpagesthatsuck.com.

TRY going on a virtual spending spree online. Visit cyberstores for all the latest in fashion, music, and books. Print pictures of what you'd buy if you could.

SKILL SET

✔ COMPUTERS

✔ MONEY

✔ WRITING

WHAT IS AN E-MERCHANT?

E-merchants sell products over the Internet. Such businesses allow customers to shop from their own homes at any time of day or night and have their purchases delivered to their doorstep.

E-commerce is a new way of doing business that's taken off in our super-charged computer world. Super e-merchants (also known as e-tailers) like Amazon.com and eBay.com have taken the retail business by storm. People spent $143.2 billion buying things online in 2005. That's a lot of cash! This has made the retail industry sit up and take notice. Even favorite retailers you find in "real" malls are starting to set up shop on the web. Toys "R" Us, Barnes and Noble, and the Gap are just a few of the traditional retailers jumping on the Internet bandwagon. Then again, so are thousands of entrepreneurial types who see an opportunity and are joining in on the fun.

What does it take to be an e-merchant? First, you have to have something to sell. It could be books, toys, clothes, computer software, airline tickets, music, or anything else you can think of. Next, you have to open a cyberstore. Not like the ones you find at the mall, but one that exists only online (and in your basement or wherever you keep your products).

The big challenge is in finding customers. To do this, you have to advertise and make your presence on the Internet known.

One of the first techniques successful e-merchants use to attract business is to make it easy for customers to buy their goods. You have to be able to accept payments online, which means credit cards. You have to provide your customers with a secure way to send you their credit card information online. When you get orders, you have to fill them and ship them. And, finally, you have to offer customer service in case things don't go exactly right.

As you can imagine, there are many different career opportunities available in e-commerce. Some entrepreneurs might take on the whole project. They might have a product or products they wish to sell, set up their own Web site, and go for it. But the chances are remote that any one person has all the skills and time necessary to run an online store alone. So a successful business might require partners or hiring others with complementary skill sets. For example, you might be a computer whiz who can design an incredible online store, process payments, and make sure credit card transactions are secure. Then you might

enlist help from someone with some retail or customer service expertise.

No matter what, make sure you choose a product that people will want to buy. Some e-merchants have gotten so excited about the technology and the possibilities of selling over the Internet that they have paid little attention to what they are selling. You can have the world's greatest Web site and get 50,000 hits a day, but if you don't have a product worth buying, you won't be in business for long.

If going it alone is not for you, there are many different job opportunities in this growing field. If you scanned employment ads in e-commerce publications, you would find technical job listings such as Internet product development and technology analyst, e-commerce technology architecture manager, e-commerce applications developers, or e-commerce infrastructure managers. These are all technical jobs that require heavy computer experience in Web development and maintenance. Some jobs may require a B.S. degree and others may require lots of experience with computer languages such as HTML, JavaScript, and Visual Basic. Some might require both.

A position like that of Internet business development manager might require a marketing or business degree and would involve research and development of sales and marketing strategies for a large e-commerce company. A director of e-commerce would probably need computer and business experience as well as an advanced degree such as an M.B.A.

Because e-commerce is such a new and evolving field, there is not one obvious choice for an education. Colleges and universities themselves are debating how to best educate their students for careers in e-commerce. Some universities offer e-commerce programs through their computer science and information science divisions. Degree programs, both undergraduate and graduate, are cropping up at business schools around the country such as the University of Texas, Duke, and Harvard. Universities are starting to realize that their students need to have diverse backgrounds in computers and business to succeed in e-commerce. With that said, a college degree is not necessarily a requirement for an e-commerce career, especially if you are great with computers.

Keep your eye on e-commerce. It is so new and is changing so quickly that you never know what exciting careers may yet develop.

☞ TRY IT OUT

ONLINE SHOPPING SPREE

Check out the Web sites of three major e-tailers online: Amazon.com (http://www.amazon.com), eToys (http://www.etoys.com), and Lands' End (http://www.landsend.com).

Surf with a purpose. Make notes about how these sites are organized. What do they have in common? What makes them stand out? What about their look is special? Is it easy to find what you are looking for? Do they offer an interesting mix of products? Can you understand how to go about buying something at the site?

GOING, GOING, GONE

Since eBay set up shop in 1995, it has become the most popular online spot in the world for practically anyone to trade practically anything. Every day more than a 100 million registered members visit the Web site (http://www.ebay.com) to buy or sell products that range from books and clothes to antiques and cars.

Do you have a special collection of something—baseball cards, stamps, dolls, or whatever? See what kinds of deals you can find on items that interest you. Clean out your closet and you may even discover a few items you're ready to get rid of. Find out from a parent if it's okay to list them on eBay. If so, ask for help figuring out how to set up your own mini-eBay shop online to sell them. The experience could provide a valuable introduction to e-commerce and you may make a little money to boot.

✔ CHECK IT OUT

🖱 ON THE WEB
VIRTUAL E-COMMERCE
Go online and go into business—virtually. Following are some fun opportunities to make your fortune—or lose it—online:

- ☼ Gazillionaire, download a free shareware copy at http://www.lavamind.com/gaz.html
- ☼ Hotshot Business at http://www.disney.go.com/hot shot/hsb.html
- ☼ Lemonade Stand Game at http://www.lemonade game.com
- ☼ Rags to Riches free concert tour game at http://www.headbone.com/wtvrags

📚 AT THE LIBRARY
FAMOUS INTERNET MERCHANTS
Read about some of the people who have made it big in e-commerce. As pioneers they have led the way in this new frontier of online shopping.

Horvitz, Leslie Alan. *Meg Whitman: President and CEO of Ebay.* New York: Ferguson, 2005.

Morales, Leslie. *Esther Dyson: Internet Visionary.* Berkeley Heights, N.J.: Enslow, 2003.

Ryan, Bernard, Jr. *Jeff Bezos: Business Executive and Founder of Amazon.com.* New York: Ferguson, 2005.

HIT THE BOOKS
Check out some of these e-commerce books to get more information about this new and exciting field:

Caraccilo, Dominic J. *E-Tailing: Careers Selling Over the Web.* New York: Rosen, 2001.

Craig, Tom. *Internet: Technology, People, Process.* North Mankato, Minn.: Smart Apple Media, 2003.

Haegle, Katie. *E-Advertising and E-Marketing: Online Opportunities.* New York: Rosen, 2001.

Lynn, Jacqueline. *Start Your Own E-Business.* Irvine, Calif.: Entrepreneur, 2005.

Scheppler, Bill. *Careers with a Click-and-Mortar Business.* New York: Rosen, 2001.

WITH THE EXPERTS

CommerceNet
169 University Avenue
Palo Alto, CA 94301-1633
http://www.commerce.net

National Retail Federation Shop.org
325 7th Street NW, Suite 1100
Washington, DC 20004-2818
http://www.nrf.com

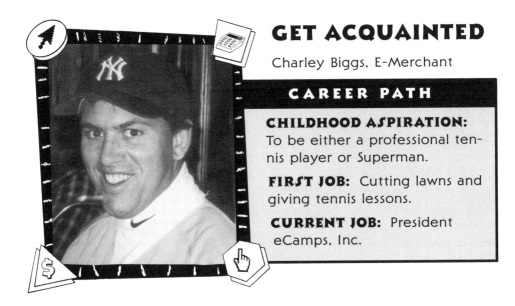

GET ACQUAINTED

Charley Biggs, E-Merchant

CAREER PATH

CHILDHOOD ASPIRATION: To be either a professional tennis player or Superman.

FIRST JOB: Cutting lawns and giving tennis lessons.

CURRENT JOB: President eCamps, Inc.

SPORTS WITH A TWIST

Charley Biggs loves playing tennis and had hopes of becoming a professional player someday. But by the time he got to college, he realized he wasn't going to make it. He pursued a degree in liberal arts because that allowed him to study many subjects. While in college, he spent the summers teaching at tennis camps.

Wall Street was the first stop on his "official" career journey. He spent two years there as a stockbroker, enjoying the work and the pace—for a while.

Then a family friend asked Briggs to work with his new business operating sports camps. The idea was to set up top-notch sports camps all over the country in many different sports. It sounded like a winner to Biggs. So he packed his bags and moved across the country to San Francisco to give it a whirl.

He started out at the bottom of the business. Answering phones and registering kids for camps were his primary duties at first. Then he moved up the ladder to take charge of a couple of camps. He did a good job and moved up to take charge of an entire sport—basketball at one point and lacrosse at another. He did a little bit of everything to run several camps in several states, including buying equipment and finding sponsors, locating great facilities, hiring directors, and finding kids to fill the camps! It was like running a business within a business and gave Biggs some great management experience. And, best of all, it gave him a chance to indulge his passion for sports.

TAKE IT TO THE NET

A business operating many sports camps is made for e-commerce. The same types of people who enrolled in the camps also used computers. The business could reach a national audience with the Internet and could make it easy for people to register for camps online.

Biggs put the business online early in the game, using a basic informational Web site. Through the years, Biggs updated the site with pictures, testimonials, a camp store, and full descriptions of camps in hundreds of locations. Online registrations doubled every year for several years as they improved their Web site.

GOING FOR THE GOAL

With this successful experience, Biggs felt ready to start his own company, eCamps Inc. He applied the same concepts to starting sports camps using catchy, easy-to-remember Web site addresses. For tennis, Biggs chose http://www. tenniscamper.com; for lacrosse, http://www.LaxCamps.com; and for field hockey, http://www.FHcamps.com. Thousands of young athletes improve athletic skills and have fun at his camps every summer.

THE KID CONNECTION

Looking back, Biggs says he can see some direct connections between what he enjoyed doing as a kid and what he's doing now. There's the sports aspect, of course. But Biggs also says that whenever he wasn't playing tennis, he was reading. He loved to read then and he loves to read now. It helps keep him on top of all the changes in the industry.

Biggs thinks the best thing you can do for your career is to have fun. Find something you enjoy and it will bring out the best in you, giving you the best shot at success.

Geographer

TAKE A TRIP!

SKILL SET

✔ MATH

✔ COMPUTERS

✔ ADVENTURE

SHORTCUTS

GO to the library, compare a current world atlas with one that was published 10 years ago, and see if you can find at least three "new" countries.

READ National Geographic magazine (http://www.nationalgeographic.com).

TRY finding all the states on a United States map and naming each state capital.

WHAT IS A GEOGRAPHER?

A geographer is a scientist who deals with the earth and its life—especially the description of the land, sea, and air, and the distribution of plant and animal life, including humans and their industries—with reference to the mutual relations of these diverse elements. Hmmm . . . that's a mouthful. Essentially it boils down to this: geographers study places and people and how the two interact with each other.

According to the Association of American Geographers, you can get a good idea if you'd like working as a geographer by taking this "Is Geography for Me?" quiz:

- ☼ Are you curious about places?
- ☼ Do you like to study maps?
- ☼ Do you prefer the window seat on airplanes?
- ☼ Are you interested in foreign areas?
- ☼ Do you like to work outside?
- ☼ Are you a problem solver?
- ☼ Are you good at seeing connections among seem- ingly unrelated processes?
- ☼ Can you adapt to rapid technological change?
- ☼ Do you try to see the big picture?
- ☼ Are you interested in the connections between humans and the environment?

If you answer yes to most of these questions, you may want to give a career in geography serious consideration. As a geographer, there are many different ways to apply your skills. For example, regional geographers become experts in major regions of the world, such as the Middle East or Europe, and may work for a government agency or in international business.

Environmental geographers focus on how humans use the earth. They might specialize in areas such as toxic waste, air pollution, and energy issues. Some of the places these geographers might work include a national park, a state department of environmental protection, or the federal Environmental Protection Agency.

Economic geography is another area of specialization for geographers. This area focuses on issues such as industry, business, transportation, trade, and the changing value of real estate. You'll find economic geographers employed by many types of companies, especially those that do business in more than one country. They work in marketing firms and in large real estate companies and banks. They also serve as traffic managers for companies that must ship their goods to lots of places.

Two of the most rapidly growing areas of geographic work involve cartography and geographic information systems (GIS). Cartography is the science of making maps, and GIS are highly sophisticated computer programs that can store, display, analyze, and map information. Geographers who specialize in cartography or GIS might work for government agencies such as the Census Bureau or the U.S. Geological Survey, or they might be employed by businesses such as telephone companies or real estate developers.

While geographers need a well-rounded educational background and a college degree in geography, they should also prepare themselves for specific demands. For instance, a regional geographer will probably need to be fluent in a second language, while a cartographer will need well-developed computer skills.

Earning a college degree in geography is a great way to open doors to all kinds of opportunities. Don't be surprised, however, to find out that few professionals who practice geography are actually called geographers. Instead, depending on their area of specialization, job titles might include area specialist, cartographer, environmental manager, and zoning inspector. So, if you aced the "Is Geography for Me?" quiz, you still need to explore the many ways of making geography an exciting part of your career.

TODAY'S LESSON IS . . .

According to the National Council for Geographic Education and the Association of American Geographers, the study of geography (and the work of geographers) can be summed up in five themes. Following are brief descriptions of each theme along with an "assignment" for putting each theme to use:

1. **Location:** No matter where you are on Earth, that spot is marked by an imaginary grid of lines called latitude and longitude. Geographers use longitude and latitude to communicate precisely and accurately where a particular place is located.

    Put this theme to work by using a map to find the latitude and longitude of the place where you live. See if you can also find the spot on Earth that is exactly opposite from your location.

2. **Place:** In order to paint verbal pictures of a particular place, geographers describe them by their physi-

cal and human characteristics. These characteristics might include language, religion, and the types of work available, as well as the surrounding landscape and the surrounding buildings.

Put this theme to work by describing the "place" surrounding your school. Make a list of all the characteristics that make it unique and compare it with a list describing a rival school across town or nearby.

3. **Human and Environmental Interaction:** In order to plan and manage the environment wisely, geographers study the ways in which humans interact with their environment.

Put this theme to work by talking to someone who has lived in your area for 25 years or more and ask him or her to describe how things have changed over the years.

4. **Movement:** All people are in connection with, and dependent on, other regions, cultures, and people in the world. Interaction among all kinds of people takes place every day as people travel, communicate with one another, and rely on one another for products, information, and ideas.

Put this theme to work by using the yellow pages in the phone book to look up restaurants. Make a list of all the different kinds of ethnic groups represented by the various restaurants. At the very least, your list should include Chinese, Mexican, and Italian. Choose one country and use an encyclopedia to find out all you can about it. Try to find some connection between the country and the type of food it is known for. For instance, if rice is known as a main staple of the cuisine, is it also known as a major export for that country?

5. **Regions:** Regions are areas in the world that are defined by certain unifying physical, human, or cultural characteristics. Geographers study how regions change over time.

Put this theme to work by using a map to divide the United States into regions based on your ideas about the physical, human, or cultural characteristics of the area. For instance, you might put all the states west of the Mississippi River and east of the Rocky Mountains into a region and you might put the states that border the Atlantic Ocean into another region. If it's your own map and it's OK to write on it, use a marker to indicate each region and write three words or phrases that describe each region.

For more information and activities involving these themes, visit National Geographic's geography education Web site at http://www.nationalgeographic.com/resources/ngo/education/themes.html.

☞ TRY IT OUT

MATT'S TOP TEN

To see more of the world than you ever dreamed possible, all you need is a computer with a connection to the Internet. Start your worldwide globe-trotting at the following top 10 online destinations chosen by the About.com Web site's in-the-know geography guide, Matt Rosenberg (see interview on page 76):

- CIA World Factbook at http://geography.about. com/library/cia/blcindex.htm
- Flags of the World at http://www.crwflags. com/fotw/flags
- Geography at About.com at http://geography. about.com
- GeoHive Global Statistics at http://www.xist.org
- Google Local at http://local.google.com
- LiveScience at http://www.livescience.com
- Nation Master at http://www.nationmaster.com
- Perry-Castañeda Library Map Collection at http:// www.lib.utexas.edu/maps
- World Climate at http://www.worldclimate.com
- World Time Zone at http://www.worldtimezone. com

✔ CHECK IT OUT

🖱 ON THE WEB

WONDERS TIMES SEVEN

Have you ever heard of the Seven Wonders of the World? You can get a firsthand look at both the ancient wonders and the modern versions by going to http://ce.eng.usf.edu/pharos/wonders.

While you're there, compare the lists and compile your own version based on which you think are the most spectacular. Print out pictures of each site and make a poster depicting your choices for an all-time seven wonders list. Feel free to add new locations that you think merit the distinction.

MAPS 101

Thanks to the ingenuity of the U.S. Geological Survey, you can become an expert on reading and making maps via the Internet. Go to the Exploring Maps Web site at http://interactive2.usgs.gov/learningweb/teachers/exploremaps.htm and work your way through activities on location, navigation, information, and exploration.

GEOGRAPHY BEE BUZZ

The National Geographic Society sponsors an annual Geography Bee to get students in grades four through eight interested in geography. National winners of the Geography Bee receive college scholarships.

To practice your spelling and find out more go online to http://www.nationalgeographic.com/geobee.

📚 AT THE LIBRARY

BOOK A WORLDWIDE TOUR

Explore the world from the comfort of the coziest chair in your house with books like these:

Bentley, Diane, and Sarah Warburton. *Seven Wonders of the Ancient World.* New York: Oxford University Press, 2005.

Gough, Barry M. *Geography and Exploration: Biographical Portraits.* Farmington Hills, Mich.: Charles Scribner's Sons, 2001.

Parsons, Jayne. *Geography of the World.* New York: DK Children's, 2006.

Wojtanik, Andrew. *Afghanistan to Zimbabwe: Country Facts that Helped Me Win the National Geographic Bee.* Washington, D.C.: National Geographic Children's Books, 2005.

 WITH THE EXPERTS

Association of American
  Geographers
1710 16th Street NW
Washington, DC 20009-3198
http://www.aag.org

Center for Geographic
  Education
San Jose State University
San Jose, CA 95192-0116
http://www2.sjsu.edu/depts/cge

National Geographic Society
1145 17th Street NW
Washington, DC 20036-4688
http://www.nationalgeographic.
  com

United States Geological Survey
12201 Sunrise Valley Drive
Herndon, VA 20192-0002
http://www.usgs.gov

GET ACQUAINTED

Matt Rosenberg, Geographer

CAREER PATH

CHILDHOOD ASPIRATION:
To be a policeman, fireman, or reporter.

FIRST JOB: Student assistant in a university library.

CURRENT JOB: Author, webmaster for an online geography site, and geography college instructor.

A CHANGE IN PLANS

Matt Rosenberg has always been fascinated by geography. He just didn't know it for a long time. Even as a young child, he was fascinated by maps and spent lots of time exploring his neighborhood. Sometimes he'd even sketch maps of the rural areas around his home.

The first time he encountered an official geography class was in his first year of college. When he enrolled in college, he fully intended to become a doctor. He signed up for an introduction to urban and economical geography course just to fulfill a general education requirement, so he was surprised when the class opened up a whole new world to him—literally. He'd never heard of geography as a career, let alone considered it for himself. Just one class, however, and he was hooked. He promptly changed his major to geography and ended up changing his destiny.

A JUGGLING ACT

Rosenberg loves geography. It's more than a profession to him; it's a passion. His enthusiasm for the subject is apparent in all the ways Rosenberg makes geography a part of his life. When it comes right down to it, Rosenberg wears several different geography hats.

One hat is as resident expert for a very popular geography Web site. Rosenberg is the geography guide for the About. com geography site at http://geography.about.com. In this role, he spends 10 to 20 hours a week researching and writing articles about all kinds of geography-related topics. One week it could be avalanches, while another week it might be the world's political distribution. He also searches the Internet to find sites of interest to geographers and manages a geography chat room.

This role has provided all kinds of opportunities for Rosenberg. One of the nicest (and most surprising!) opportunities came when he received an e-mail message from a book editor asking him to write a book about geography. This opportunity resulted in a new geography hat for Rosenberg to wear: that of author. So far he's written two books: *The Handy Geography Answer Book* (Farmington Hills, Mich.: Visible Ink, 1998) and *The Geography Bee Complete Preparation Handbook* (New York: Three Rivers, 2002).

For several years, he worked as director of emergency services for the American Red Cross in Southern California. He says his geographical skills helped him prepare for and respond to disasters all over the world involving earthquakes, floods, and hurricanes.

Now, having recently completed his master's degree in geography, he'll be adding another hat to his repertoire by teaching geography at a local college. In addition, he is a member of the Association of American Geographers and the National Council for Geographic Education.

A FEW SUGGESTIONS

If you are considering a career in geography, Rosenberg has a few suggestions for you.

First of all, be curious. Read the newspaper and watch the news to find out what's happening in the world. Look at maps. Rosenberg says that future geographers should learn to use a world atlas the same way other people use a dictionary. When you hear about a place you aren't familiar with, look it up!

Second, be an explorer. Start noticing where you are and what it's like. Observe your environment and make observations about it. Looking is one thing, but understanding is another. Make sure you do both.

And, finally, when you get to high school, find out if your school offers an advanced placement (AP) geography course. If it does, take it and get a good introduction to what the field is all about. Plus, you'll get a chance to earn college credit while you're still in high school.

International Trade Specialist

SKILL SET

✔ TRAVEL

✔ MONEY

✔ ADVENTURE

SHORTCUTS

GO host a foreign exchange student or become one yourself when you get old enough. But get your parents' permission first!

READ everything you can find about other places and peoples. Keep up with current events to learn about history in the making.

TRY eating out at a restaurant that specializes in food from another country such as Thailand, Vietnam, or Ireland.

WHAT IS AN INTERNATIONAL TRADE SPECIALIST?

Traveling the globe in search of exotic products to sell at home can be one of the glamorous perks of being an international trade specialist. An international trade specialist is either an importer (someone who brings products into a country) or an exporter (someone who sells products in other countries) or both. The United States trades goods with countries all over the world. Some of the biggest United States trading partners are Canada, Japan, Germany, the United Kingdom, France, and Mexico.

Exporting any type of product involves handling lots of details. Researching potential markets, making contact with companies in foreign countries who will sell their products, dealing with foreign governments, and preparing goods to be shipped overseas are typical parts of a day's work for an international trade specialist. Dealing with customs and all the rules and regulations in each country is another big part of this job.

Importers also deal with foreign governments, customs, and shipping. Their job is to identify products that are likely to be a big hit in their home country. Then they negotiate good prices and make efforts to get the products to their country. They often take "shopping" trips to different countries in search of special items that other people will want to buy. Good taste and an eye for what sells are important for an importer.

Sometimes international trade specialists work for major corporations such as Coca-Cola, Nike, and IBM. Companies like these export their products to foreign markets and hire international trade specialists to get the job done. They may also import various materials or depend on international partners to provide labor to produce certain products.

Other international trade specialists are self-employed businesspeople who either sell products to other countries or import goods to sell in their countries. They may own a specialty shop (or shops) and scour the world for special products to sell, or they may specialize in a certain type of product such as jewelry or exotic foods that they provide to other clients. Sometimes these entrepreneurs have a background in international trade, and sometimes they just come across a great product or have the "perfect" idea and decide to make a go of it. Either way, there's lots to learn.

Training such as that offered by the U.S. Department of Commerce's International Trade Administration often means the difference between growing a business or failing. Good communication skills are a must for an international trade specialist, and fluency in more than one language, while not an absolute requirement, is helpful. International trade specialists must be knowledgeable about the legal requirements of their home countries as well as the other countries they are dealing with. Some international trade specialists have a legal background, which can prove extremely useful.

A good international trade specialist has to be a problem solver too. Things do not always go smoothly when products are being shipped thousands of miles away and foreign governments are involved. Oceans, equipment, language barriers, current events, and all kinds of obstacles can conspire to wreak havoc on even the best-laid plans. When things go badly, diplomacy is the key to sorting things out.

Some international trade specialists actually live in foreign countries. Such experience can be beneficial for people who are flexible and willing to adapt to local conditions and customs. They must keep up on political and economic conditions that might affect their ability to do business.

Several different paths can lead you to a career in world trade. Many universities offer undergraduate degrees and master's programs in international business. These programs often include specialties in different regions of the world and intense foreign language study as well as international business courses in which students learn the details of doing business in other countries. Some require that you work in a foreign country for six months as an intern. This valuable experience can give you a foot in the door when you are looking for that first job.

To increase your chances of landing a job in international trade, get a college degree in business, law, or accounting, and don't forget the foreign language. Also, seriously consider an advanced degree in international business.

Another way to add an international flair to your career path is to become a foreign exchange trader. This isn't a field you jump into without specialized training, but it can be rewarding and financially lucrative as well. A foreign exchange trader basically trades currency or money between different countries. It probably sounds easier than it is. This is an exciting but risky career as just one transaction can involve millions of dollars! Foreign exchange traders often have degrees in economics, mathematics, or statistics. It's a field to look into if a finance-related career in international business sounds interesting to you.

All in all, a career in international trade can offer plenty of travel and adventure. But it also requires lots of hard work and business skills to get those products where they need to go.

☞ TRY IT OUT

TALK THE TALK
Impress yourself with your foreign language abilities by going online to Foreignword (http://www.foreignword.com), an online dictionary and translation tool. Make a list of 10 favorite (or random!) words. Then translate the word into at least three different languages using the translation tool. Compare the results. Are the words similar in any ways?

Another fun way to build your international vocabulary is at the Traveling Word of the Day Web site at http://www.travlang.com/wordofday. Each day you can hear a new word or phrase translated into 50 different languages.

SHOPPING SLEUTH
Next time you go to a mall or department store take along a notepad and pen. Snoop around the product labels and see if you can find products made in China, Taiwan, Japan, Korea,

and, of course, the good ol' U.S. of A. Jot down the type of product, the name of the company, the price, and anything you notice about the quality of each product. Where do the best and most interesting products come from? Does price factor (either higher or lower) seem to be linked in any way to the origin of each product?

✔ CHECK IT OUT

🖱 ON THE WEB
GLOBE-TROTTING WITH THE CIA
Visit the CIA's World Factbook Web site at www.odci.gov/cia/publications/factbook/index.html. Here you'll find tons of "intelligence" information about every country in the world. It contains details about each country's geography, population, government, and economy, including what kind of products they import and export and what countries they do business with. Check out several countries that seem interesting to you and find out what they are trading.

GO GLOBAL
Import. Export. Global economy. Fair trade. International trade specialists encounter these issues all the time. See what you can find out about them at the following fun-filled Web sites:

- ☼ Compare the lives of two dairy farmers in very different countries at the Milking It Web site at http://www.oxfam.org.uk/coolplanet/milkingit.
- ☼ Try trading around the world with the online game found at http://www.imf.org/external/np/exr/center/students/trade.
- ☼ Where do chokky bikkies come from? And, for that matter, what is a chokky bikkie? Find out at http://www.oxfam.org.uk/coolplanet/ontheline/schools/chocbix.
- ☼ Find a variety of global games and activities at http://www.globalfootprints.org.

☼ Explore the world with Kids' World at http://www.peacecorps.gov/kids/index.html.

📚 AT THE LIBRARY

INTERNATIONAL KNOWLEDGE EXCHANGE

Learn more about world trade and the issues affecting international trade specialists in books that include:

Burgess, John. *World Trade: Exploring Business and Economics.* New York: Chelsea House, 2001.

Cooper, Adrian. *Fair Trade? A Look at the Way the World is Today.* Corona, Calif.: Stargazer Books, 2005.

Davis, Lucile. *Trade and Commerce.* Farmington Hills, Mich.: Blackbirch, 2004.

Frost, Randall, and Tim Schwartzenberger. *The Globalization of Trade.* North Mankato, Minn.: Smart Apple Media, 2003.

January, Brendon. *Globalize It!* Fairfield, Iowa: 21st Century, 2003.

Reid, Stuart. *Inventions and Trade.* North Mankato, Minn.: Thameside, 2003.

🗣 WITH THE EXPERTS

Federation of International Trade Associations
11800 Sunrise Valley Drive, Suite 210
Reston, VA 20191
http://www.fita.org

International Small Business Consortium
3309 Windjammer Street
Norman, OK 73072
http://www.isbc.com

International Trade Association
1244 North Nokomis NE
Alexandria, MN 56308
http://www.expertpages.com/org/ita.htm

GET ACQUAINTED

Susan Gravely,
International Trade Specialist

CAREER PATH

CHILDHOOD ASPIRATION: To be the wife of an ambassador.

FIRST JOB: Wrapping presents in an upscale clothing store.

CURRENT JOB: President of Vietri, an Italian dinnerware and accessories import company.

READY FOR ANYTHING

When Susan Gravely was a young girl, her favorite movie was *Gone With the Wind.* She admits it sounds kind of weird, but her favorite character was Mammy, the family's maid. Gravely recognized that Mammy was a really good person who got a lot done, and she wanted to grow up to be just like her.

She also remembers finding her father's work in international business fascinating. She loved entertaining people from all over the world in their home. She discovered if she volunteered to help serve the drinks, she could sit in on all the interesting conversations.

But Gravely was raised during a time when society didn't have many career expectations for women. The general idea was for women to marry successful men and let them take care of earning the money. Even so, Gravely always had a feeling that she wanted to provide for herself.

And, in a way, her life prepared her for success on her own by teaching her how to work hard. Whether it was running a lemonade stand, baby-sitting, or volunteering with her church group, Gravely was always busy doing something. Even as a Girl Scout, she enjoyed working toward new badges.

A HOLIDAY TO REMEMBER

Although Gravely never intended to become president of a wildly successful company, there are some common themes in her work that brought her to this place. Color, people, and building things have made frequent appearances in many of the job choices she's made along the way.

After college, she took a job with an architectural firm. Then she started designing play spaces for sick children at hospitals and doctors' offices. Then she helped a friend open three retail stores. But things started really coming together when she took a nine-month sabbatical to study interior design in New York City.

It was at this point that her mother invited Gravely and her sister on a trip to Italy's Amalfi coast. It was there that the women fell in love—with dinnerware. With nothing to lose (except, of course, their $20,000 investment), they decided to start a business importing Italian dishes. Talk about being in the right place at the right time!

Their company's product line started with some colorful and elegant dishes they traced to a factory in Vietri (hence the name of their company), and it has grown to include tableware and glassware from 40 Italian manufacturers. From the northern part of Italy, they find products made from white clay, called terra bianca, which are decorated with fruit, flowers, animals, and fish. Southern Italy offers up a dazzling array of products made from red clay, called terra–cotta. These dishes are often brightly glazed in cool yellows and blues. Some of the designs have been used since the 1300s and have been handed down from generation to generation.

Through the years, Vietri has grown to employ 42 people in its main office and 60 sales representatives. More than 3,500 better gift stores and retail stores in the United States carry Vietri's products.

As president of the company, Gravely makes about four trips to Italy every year to meet with manufacturers and designers. She also visits places such as France and Germany for inspiration. Gravely considers the travel to be one of the best parts of running an international business. She appreciates the real friendships she has found in working with the Italian merchants and artisans.

A SIMPLE PLAN

At this point, Gravely has realized that you can't make everything happen in your life. There's only so much you actually do, so that's why making good choices is so important. Gravely has decided that the best thing she can do now is enjoy her family and work hard.

Gravely says that success seems to follow when her focus is on making her business the best it can be. Loving her work, keeping the right balance between work and her family responsibilities, and finding free time to enjoy the people and projects she most cares about—now that's Gravely's idea of a *vita bellissimo* (beautiful life).

Lawyer

WHAT IS A LAWYER?

The main thing that any type of lawyer does is to advise people or businesses about legal matters and to act as their advocate in legal affairs. Most lawyers (also known as attorneys) specialize in either criminal or civil law. There are two sides to criminal law: the defense and the prosecution. Defense attorneys represent someone who is accused of a crime in trial proceedings. Prosecutors, often working through a state or federal district attorney's office, represent the "people" in bringing charges against a suspected criminal. You've probably seen shows on television that depict how these two sides of the legal system work.

On the civil side, a lawyer may specialize in a certain kind of law such as family law, real estate, tax law, trusts, wills, and other legal matters. A particularly hot area for civil attorneys is corporate law. These types of lawyers may specialize in a wide range of business issues, including corporate financing, contracts, acquisitions, bankruptcy, and employee benefits. The objective is to get deals done legally so that problems don't arise in the future.

The other kind of corporate law deals with the problems that do come up. These kinds of attorneys are often called litigators, and they represent corporate clients who are dealing with potential problems such as breaches of contract, class-action lawsuits, and white-collar crime.

For better or worse, lawsuits have become more common in our society. As if crime alone couldn't account for enough legal activity, law now plays a part in virtually every part of business and, in many ways, life in general. For example, if someone slips on the ice in front of your house, he or she may have grounds to sue you. Big areas of growth in legal action involve areas such as employee benefits, health care, intellectual property, sexual harassment, the environment, and real estate.

If you watch any law shows on TV, you may get the idea that lawyers spend most of their time at court, arguing cases before a judge and jury. Not so. Even if their work does involve court appearances, and some lawyers rarely even step inside a courtroom, most lawyers' time is spent in a law library doing research or sitting behind a computer writing contracts, briefs, and other types of legal documentation. All this homework can make the difference between winning or losing a case.

One of the biggest challenges a potential lawyer faces is getting into law school. Since there are so many applications from aspiring lawyers, law schools can be particular about

who they pick. Good (make that excellent) grades in college are vital. There is no absolute "prelaw" major but many law students find a background in political science, government, history, economics, or business to be helpful. What's important is a major that provides plenty of opportunity to hone skills in writing, reading, thinking logically, and communicating effectively. Law school applicants must also pass the LSAT (law school admission test).

For those lucky enough to make it into law school and to successfully complete three years of study there, the next big hurdle is passing the bar exam. Each state issues its own version of this really tough, six-hour-long test. The exam is so challenging that many students take special classes just to prepare for it, study for months, and still end up having to take it more than once before they pass.

When it's time to find a job, most lawyers either open their own private practice or join a law firm. Others find jobs either with a local government or in federal agencies such as the Department of Justice, the Treasury Department, or the Department of Defense. The rest are employed as house counsel by business firms, religious groups, or nonprofit organizations.

If the pursuit of justice is something you care about and you think you're ready to handle some tough questions, consider law as a career in which you can make a difference.

☞ TRY IT OUT

YOU BE THE JUDGE

For a fascinating—and fun—look at a streamlined version of the court system in the real world, visit http://www.icourt house.com. Here you can be a juror, view the evidence, and present your case online. Or participate in a mock trial where you decide if White Star Line, operators of the ill-fated ship Titanic, was to blame for the ship's sinking at http://www. andersonkill.com/titanic/home.htm.

And the verdict is . . .

EASY LEGALESE

Like any profession, law comes with its own vocabulary, sometimes known as "legalese." Visit Law.com's legal lingo dictionary at http://www.dictionary.law.com.asp to find out what some of the following terms mean:

- ☼ Act of God
- ☼ Arraignment
- ☼ Brief
- ☼ Cop a plea
- ☼ Due process
- ☼ Good Samaritan law
- ☼ Hung jury
- ☼ Pro bono
- ☼ Quid pro quo
- ☼ Taking the fifth

✔ CHECK IT OUT

🖰 ON THE WEB

GET YOUR FEET WET

Jump into some of the following Web sites and get your feet wet learning things about government and law that lawyers need to know:

- ☼ Demand justice for kids and youth at http://www.usdoj.gov/kidspage.
- ☼ Get up close and personal with the Constitution of the United States at http://www.archives.gov/national-archives-experience/charters/constitution.html.
- ☼ Let Ben guide you to some fascinating online finds at http://bensguide.gpo.gov/9-12/index.html.
- ☼ Learn about staying on the right side of the law at http://www.lawforkids.org.

☼ Go inside the courtroom at http://www.usdoj.gov/usao/eousa/kidspage/index.html.

WHO'S WHO IN LAW

Law firms come in all shapes and sizes. Some are private practices run by just one attorney, while others are major firms employing thousands of lawyers in offices all over the world. To find out which law firms thousands of attorneys say are the best, go online to see the results of the Vault Top Law Firm survey at http://www.vault.com/nr/lawrankings.jsp.

What kinds of clients are these firms likely to serve? Do you think you'd like to work for a firm like one of these? Why or why not?

AT THE LIBRARY

THROW THE BOOK AT YOUR CAREER

Here are some books that can give you more ideas about a lawful future:

Bell-Rehwoldt, Sheri. *Law: Careers for the Twenty-First Century.* Farmington Hills, Mich.: Lucent Books, 2005.

Dejohn, Heather, and Lois Lewis. *The Chief Justice of the Supreme Court.* Farmington Hills, Mich.: Blackbirch, 2002.

Emert, Phyllis Raybin. *Attorneys General: Enforcing the Law.* Minneapolis: Oliver, 2005.

Parks, Peggy J. *Lawyer: Exploring Careers.* Farmington Hills, Mich.: KidHaven, 2003.

Wheeler, Jill C. *Thurgood Marshall.* Edina, Minn.: Abdo and Daughters, 2003.

WITH THE EXPERTS

American Bar Association
321 North Clark Street
Chicago, IL 60610-4714
http://www.abanet.org

Association of Corporate Counsel
1025 Connecticut Avenue NW, Suite 200
Washington, DC 20036-5425
http://www.acca.com

Association of Trial Lawyers of America
1050 31 Street NW
Washington, DC 20007-4405
http://www.atlanet.org

GET ACQUAINTED

Cynthia Tucker, Attorney

CAREER PATH

CHILDHOOD ASPIRATION:
Toyed with different ideas at different times. Thought about being a teacher and considered trying to fulfill her mother's dream of singing on Broadway but reconsidered when she realized that she couldn't sing!

FIRST JOB: Flight attendant for international airlines.

CURRENT JOB: Commissioner of Massachusetts Commission Against Discrimination and general practice attorney.

A FAMILY AFFAIR

Cynthia Tucker grew up in a family of seven children. Her father was the first black bus driver in her hometown of Springfield, Massachusetts. Tucker was just 12 years old when her dad died, leaving her mom to raise and support the family on her own. Tucker is still not sure how her mom managed to do that and put all seven children through college on her earnings from running a beauty salon in their home. Tucker remembers that her mother worked from sunup to sundown and always wanted a better life for her children. Today three of the seven kids are lawyers, one of them is a doctor, one is an educational counselor, and the other two are in business.

AROUND THE WORLD AND BACK

Law wasn't Tucker's first choice for a career. In college, she majored in sociology and assumed she'd pursue a career in social work. A couple of unrelated circumstances changed everything for her. Tucker's first experience with the law came through some work she did with the American Civil Liberties Union on a project that examined the hiring practices at local television stations. Although her participation was strictly from a sociological standpoint, she was intrigued with the legal aspects of the project.

Her second exposure to legal ideas came about after college when she went to work as an international flight attendant. While traveling around the world, Tucker became fascinated with international law and treaties. She also discovered that she got airsick a lot, which made working as a flight attendant not such a good career choice for her.

FLYING IN A NEW DIRECTION

Next stop for Tucker's career was law school, which she describes as a "relentless" experience in learning. It takes a lot of reading and research to cultivate a legal mind, and Tucker worked hard to complete the program—even after marrying and having a child.

If law school was tough, passing the bar exam proved even tougher. Tucker didn't pass it the first time, but she was determined to get it right no matter what. Keeping an eye on her goal and maintaining her focus, Tucker's perseverance paid off.

While pursuing acceptance by the bar, Tucker worked as a legislative aide for a state senator. The work involved drafting new legislation and was something Tucker enjoyed for several years.

SETTING UP SHOP

For many years, Tucker worked out of her own general practice law firm. General practice means that Tucker did a little bit of everything. Family law, real estate, and personal injury are areas that kept her busy. She still does this on a limited basis.

However, in 2000, Tucker was appointed Commissioner of the Massachusetts Commission Against Discrimination (MCAD) by the governor. In this capacity she acts as an administrative judge overseeing thousands of discrimination cases filed annually throughout the state.

Tucker says that recognizing that laws, and by extension lawyers, impact every aspect of life is a critically important position to hold in our society. As such, pursuing justice has to be about more than just winning.

THE ROAD TO SUCCESS

Success will come, says Tucker, when someone enjoys his or her work, stays motivated, and finds passion in what he or she is doing. She advises young people to "be involved and be actively patient" in whatever it is that interests them. You can't just sit around waiting for success to come your way. Stay active, and change will come. The road to success is paved by your good deeds, Tucker believes. She says that if you only measure success by how much money lawyers make you don't recognize the true and full meaning of the rule of law.

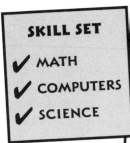

TAKE A TRIP!

Manufacturing Engineer

SHORTCUTS

SKILL SET

✔ MATH

✔ COMPUTERS

✔ SCIENCE

GO visit a plant where any kind of product is made to see the manufacturing process in action.

READ all you can about inventors and their inventions.

TRY building a really complex structure with LEGOs.

WHAT IS A MANUFACTURING ENGINEER?

A manufacturing engineer designs machines and processes that do things more quickly and with greater ease than humans could do them. This practice is called *automation*, and it's the cornerstone of the manufacturing process. A manufacturing engineer starts with 200 basic manufacturing processes and more than 40,000 materials, and with these tools, he or she develops ways of making products that range in sophistication from chocolate chip cookies to jet fighters.

Sometimes manufacturing engineers develop processes to manufacture new products, and sometimes they develop new ways to manufacture already existing products. Other times manufacturing engineers devote their time to keeping manufacturing systems running smoothly, dealing with the vendors who provide the materials needed in manufacturing, and fine-tuning various manufacturing functions. Whether it's starting something new or maintaining an existing process, manufacturing engineers make sure their systems are safe, reliable, efficient, and productive. To do their jobs, manufacturing engineers rely on a combination of scientific and mathematical knowledge and experience, as well as good judgment and common sense.

Manufacturing Engineer

Manufacturing engineers generally have at least a bachelor's degree in mechanical, electrical, or chemical engineering. This type of educational background, coupled with some experience, prepares them to take the lead in many types of manufacturing situations. Manufacturing engineers work in virtually any kind of industry that produces tangible products. Telecommunications, computer science, and other high-tech industries are currently hot areas of innovation in manufacturing; however, manufacturing engineers can be found in factories and plants that make anything from toilet paper or pencils to candy and soda.

Access to this profession can also be earned through a two-year degree in engineering technology. Engineering technicians get into the workplace and into the thick of things quicker, but the trade-off comes with fewer on-the-job responsibilities and lower pay. Technicians are part of a team under the guidance of full-fledged engineers and other types of professionals. It's an option to consider if you want to use your knowledge of math and science to solve real-life problems but don't want to pursue a four-year college degree just yet.

According to the American Society for Engineering Education (ASEE), there are a few questions you can ask yourself to find out if engineering might be a good career choice for you. These questions are

- ☼ Do you get good grades in math and science?
- ☼ Do you enjoy knowing how things work?
- ☼ Do you ever think of new or better ways to do things?
- ☼ If you get a gift that requires some assembly, do you put it together yourself?
- ☼ Do you like to work with computers and play video games?
- ☼ Do you like to do mazes and jigsaw puzzles?
- ☼ Do you usually make sound decisions, and do people trust your judgment?
- ☼ Can you express yourself easily and clearly?
- ☼ Do you work well with others?
- ☼ Do you like to know "why"?

If you answered yes to several of these questions, the ASEE says that your potential for success in engineering could be high. Of course, there's still plenty of time to work on communication skills, math and science grades, and the like. Start now to give yourself the best chance for success in this profession by taking as many math and science classes as you can. Work hard to get good grades, because that's the best way to get your foot in the door for an engineering career.

☞ TRY IT OUT

WHERE DID IT COME FROM?

Pick a product, any product, and trace its origins from beginning to end. For instance, say you choose a book like this one. You'd need to start the manufacturing process all the way back in the forest with the trees that were cut to make the paper. Then you'd move forward step by step.

Make a chart showing the entire process that you've chosen. Use library and Internet resources as well as your own common sense to figure out the manufacturing process.

HOORAY FOR ENGINEERS!

What do Thomas Edison, Henry Ford, Alexander Graham Bell, Eli Whitney, and Grace Murray Hopper have in common? They were all engineers known for famous inventions. Use information you find about people like these and others to create your own guide to great engineers. Keep the information in a notebook, file, or box so you can continue to add new entries.

Places to look for information include the Internet—searching a specific name or the words "famous engineers" or "famous inventors"—and books such as:

St. George, Judith. *So You Want to be an Inventor?* New York: Penguin, 2005.

Williams, Marcia. *Hooray for Inventors*. Cambridge, Mass.: Candlewick, 2005.

✔ CHECK IT OUT

🖱 ON THE WEB

VIRTUAL MANUFACTURING

All it takes is a computer linked to the Internet to get a look at several different kinds of manufacturing processes. Visit the following Web sites for a birds-eye view of how some of your favorite products are made:

- ☼ See for yourself how all kinds of everyday things are made at http://manufacturing.stanford.edu.
- ☼ Find links to over 90 virtual plant tours on the Internet at http://bradley.bradley.edu/rf/plantour.htm.
- ☼ Make sure to stop by the Manufacturing is Cool Web site at http://www.manufacturingiscool.com.

☼ Get Tech at the National Association of Manufacturers Web site for kids at http://www.gettech.org.
☼ If you can dream it, you can do it or at least find out
   how at http://www.dreamit-doit.com.

And to look "under the hood" of everything from automo-
biles to electronics, visit the awesome How Stuff Works Web
site at http://howstuffworks.com or the kid-sized version at
http://www.express.howstuffworks.com.

📚 AT THE LIBRARY

MAKE IT HAPPEN

Making stuff happen is what manufacturing is all about. Read
amazing accounts of how your favorite products get made
in books such as:

———————

Axelrod, Karen. *Watch It Made in the USA: A Visitor's Guide
to the Companies that Make Your Favorite Products.* New
York: Avalon, 2002.

Briscoe, Diana. *Bridge Building: Bridge Designs and How
They Work.* Mankato, Minn.: Capstone, 2005.

Englart, Mindi. *Made in USA: Bikes.* Farmington Hills, Mich.:
Blackbirch, 2002.

———. *Made in USA: Helicopters.* Farmington Hills, Mich.:
Blackbirch, 2002.

Howard, Devon. *Made in USA: Skateboards.* Farmington Hills,
Mich.: Blackbirch, 2005.

Kreger, Claire. *Made in USA: Homes.* Farmington Hills, Mich.:
Blackbirch, 2003.

Royston, Angela. *How Is a Soccer Ball Made?* Chicago: Heinemann Library, 2005.

———. *How Is a T-shirt Made?* Chicago: Heinemann Library,
2006.

Smith, Ryan. *Golf Balls from Start to Finish.* Farmington Hills,
Mich.: Blackbirch, 2005.

Stone, Tanya Lee. *Made in USA: Toothpaste.* Farmington Hills,
Mich.: Blackbirch, 2001.

Woods, Samuel G. *Pogo Sticks: From Start to Finish.* Farmington Hills, Mich.: Blackbirch, 2001.

———————

HANDS-ON READING

To find out if you have the right stuff to become an engineer, try some of the projects in the following books:

Adams, Richard Craig. *Engineering Projects for Young Scientists*. Danbury, Conn.: Franklin Watts, 2001.

Haslam, Andrew, and David Glover. *Building: Make It Work*. Minnetonka, Minn.: Two Can, 2001.

———. *Machines: Make It Work*. Minnetonka, Minn.: Two Can, 2000.

For those of you not quite ready for building bridges and working with robots, try your hand at paper engineering. Following are books jam-packed with project ideas:

Birmingham, Duncan. *Pop Up! A Manual of Paper Mechanisms*. Miami: Tarquin, 1999.

Carter, David, and James Diaz. *Elements of Pop-Up: A Pop-Up Book for Aspiring Paper Engineers*. New York: Little Simon, 1999.

———. *Let's Make It Pop Up!* New York: Little Simon, 2004.

WITH THE EXPERTS

American Society for Engineering Education
1818 N Street NW, Suite 600
Washington, DC 20036-2479
http://www.asee.org

Junior Engineering Technical Society (JETS)
1420 King Street, Suite 405
Alexandria, VA 22314-2750
http://www.jets.org

Society of Manufacturing Engineers
1 SME Drive
PO Box 930
Dearborn, MI 48121-2408
http://www.sme.org

Society of Women Engineers
230 East Ohio Street, Suite 400
Chicago, IL 60611-3265
http://www.swe.org

Tooling and Manufacturing Association
1177 South Dee Road
Park Ridge, IL 60068-4379
http://www.tmanet.com

GET ACQUAINTED

Jon Carver,
Manufacturing Engineer

CAREER PATH

CHILDHOOD ASPIRATION: To be an engineer.

FIRST JOB: Bag boy at a grocery store.

CURRENT JOB: Manager of equipment engineering for a major cosmetics manufacturing company.

A PERFECT FIT

Even as a boy, it was apparent that Jon Carver was destined to become an engineer. He was always curious about what made things tick and was famous in his family for tearing things apart and trying to put them back together again. Every spare minute was spent building things with his Erector Set.

When he reached high school, he ran track with a friend whose father owned a cosmetics plant. The friend helped him get a summer job working there, and Carver's education in manufacturing began with some firsthand experience.

AN INDIRECT PATH

In college. Carver decided to major in psychology instead of engineering after finding some of the engineering classes a bit boring. Although this is an unusual training choice for an engineer, Carver says that the most important thing an engineer needs to know is how to learn. He's found that as long as he knows where to find answers to problems and isn't afraid to ask technical experts for help, he's managed just fine.

LOOKING GOOD

Carver now works for a major cosmetics company that produces millions of units of more than 3,000 different products—everything from lipstick to shampoo. His job is to find equipment that automates the way these products are made and packaged as simply and inexpensively as possible.

This task often means integrating several different pieces of equipment into one production process. Once he's put together the best system he can find, he has to make sure that the equipment does what it's supposed to do and that all the equipment works well together for steps like filling, labeling, and capping. With some systems processing as many as 250 pieces a minute, you can understand how timing can be everything in this line of work.

A DAY IN THE LIFE OF A LIPSTICK

Carver and his colleagues go to an awful lot of trouble to make their customers look good. To get an idea of what's involved, consider what it takes to make a batch of lipstick.

First, the ingredients—waxes, pigments, and fragrance—are carefully mixed in huge vats. Then the vats are heated, and the mixture is blended.

Next, the lipstick mixture is poured into 5-gallon buckets and taken to the manufacturing plant where one of Carver's systems takes over. Here, the lipstick mixture is remelted and poured into molds. Once it solidifies, it's blown out into a lipstick tube.

Then it goes through a quality inspection to make sure it passes very stringent standards involving consistency and color, among other criteria. The lipsticks that pass the test move down an assembly line where machines put covers on each tube and apply labels. Farther down the line, the individual tubes of lipstick are sealed in plastic and packed into crates for shipment to customers.

ADVICE TO FUTURE MANUFACTURING ENGINEERS

According to Carver, the next generation of manufacturing engineers really has its work cut out. The challenge for future manufacturing engineers will be to create high-tech automation systems that are as cost efficient as overseas labor. Right now, the trend is to have American goods produced in other countries where labor costs tend to be lower. It will take some exceptional engineering talent to stem that tide.

If you are up for that challenge, Carver says the best way you can prepare is to get a well-rounded education. Learn as much as you can about as much as you can. A broad, diverse background will open your mind to all the possibilities!

Mathematician

SKILL SET

✔ MATH
✔ COMPUTERS
✔ SCIENCE

GO piece together a 3-D puzzle and put your math logic skills to work.

READ *Go Figure! A Totally Cool Book About Numbers* by Johnny Ball (New York: DK, 2005) for an interesting introduction to the world of numbers.

TRY making a list of all the ways math is used in everyday life. Put some thought into it and you'll come up with a very long list!

WHAT IS A MATHEMATICIAN?

Here's a career that really adds up. Mathematician is consistently ranked as one of the top five careers (on the basis of salary, benefits, outlook for the future, stress level, work environment, and job security). It is a career that offers a surprising number of options and provides challenge, discovery, and a chance to make a real difference in the world.

Simply put, mathematicians are problem solvers. They use mathematical theories and techniques along with the latest technology to solve all kinds of economic, scientific, engineering, and business problems. A mathematician might use various mathematical modeling and computational methods to figure out, for instance, the best way for an airline to schedule flights to 150 locations using 64 jets. Or they might determine the effectiveness of a new drug by analyzing data on several thousand test patients.

Some mathematicians, called *theoretical mathematicians*, enjoy discovering new mathematical rules and finding new ways to use math ideas. They are in constant pursuit of answers to their questions about why things work the way they do. They look for patterns in the world around them and get great satisfaction in giving logical proofs (evidence) to their claims. Theoretical mathematicians often teach in colleges or universities, and many now work in industrial and high-tech research labs. Their new discoveries help further important advances in science, technology, and engineering.

Other mathematicians, called *applied mathematicians*, use mathematics in practical ways to do their job. That means that they apply mathematical principles to real-life problems. Recent work has involved developing ways for people to buy products over the Internet, called electronic commerce, and achieving major advances in the ways people communicate with each other through technology such as pagers and PDAs. In addition, some mathematicians are helping biologists understand the mathematical codes found in human genes and are doing important work to crack DNA (deoxyribonucleic) codes. The applied side of mathematics can be particularly exciting because mathematicians can actually see the results of their work in new technology and new systems.

Mathematicians work in all kinds of places including business, industry, government, and education. You'll find plenty of mathematicians in the computer and the communications industries, as well as in oil companies, banks, insurance companies, security and commodity exchanges, pharmaceutical companies, and consulting firms. Mathematicians also

work for almost every branch of the federal government. Sometimes they are assigned to top-secret projects for agencies such as the Department of Defense or the National Security Agency.

Probably the single most common characteristic of a successful mathematician is curiosity. Once intrigued by a problem, a mathematician seeks to solve it with a combination of logic, intuition, and imagination, often experiencing countless rounds of bad guesses before finding the final solution.

As you might have guessed by now, becoming a mathematician requires a good education with a strong background in math. A bachelor's degree in mathematics is a must, and for many positions, it is only the starting point. You can start preparing yourself now by taking courses in algebra, geometry, and calculus. Taking these classes helps build your brain power and gets you thinking like a mathematician.

☞ TRY IT OUT

WHY STUDY MATH?
You're sitting in pre-algebra class, and your teacher is going on and on about multiple exponents. The only brain cell currently awake in your body suddenly screams, "Why do I need to know this stuff anyway?" If you've ever experienced a similar reaction to a seemingly endless math lecture, you'll want to check out some answers given by many interesting math professionals at the Web site of the Mathematical Association of America (http://www.maa.org/careers/index.html).

Snoop around a little, think a little, then ask yourself "why study math?" Make a poster to share your conclusions with the rest of the world.

IT ALL ADDS UP
Go online to the Math Forum and join students and teachers from around the world in solving math-related "problems of the week." There are creative challenges for both the elementary and middle school students in geometry, algebra,

trigonometry, and calculus. See how far you can go at http://mathforum.org and http://www.mathcounts.org.

THE DOCTOR IS IN

Have a question about math? Ask Dr. Math. This online resource includes an amazing array of math resources from the elementary level all the way through high school and beyond. Browse through an assortment of mathematical topics and see if you can stump the experts by submitting your own questions to http://mathforum.org/drmath.

CHECK IT OUT

🖰 ON THE WEB

MORE MATH FUN AND GAMES

It's as easy as one, two, three to learn more about math and add up the ways to make numbers a part of your future. Just go online to some of the following Web sites and find out for yourself:

- ☼ Read about women who have made their mark in math at http://www.agnesscott.edu/lriddle/women/women.htm.
- ☼ Treat yourself to a mathematical snack at http://www.exploratorium.edu/snacks/iconmath.html.
- ☼ Discover some fun facts about math at http://www.math.hmc.edu/funfacts.
- ☼ Assign yourself some fun math lessons at http://math.rice.edu/lanius/Lessons.
- ☼ Tease your brain with the math challenges found at http://www.eduplace.com/math/brain/index.html.
- ☼ Get friendly with math and science at http://www.gettech.org.
- ☼ Rev up your brain power and get smarter at http://getsmarter.org/index.cfm.
- ☼ Girls, help yourselves (and your futures) to some ideas and inspiration at http://www.braincake.org.

📚 AT THE LIBRARY

MAGICAL MATH

Who says math can't be fun? Try some of the activities in the following books and amaze your family and friends with your mathematical magic:

Carter, Philip, and Ken Russell. *The Complete Book of Fun Math: 250 Confidence-Boosting Tricks, Tests and Puzzles.* Indianapolis: John Wiley, 2004.

Flansburg, Scott. *Math Magic: How to Master Everyday Math Problems.* New York: Harper, 2004.

Ho, Oliver. *Amazing Math Magic.* New York: Sterling, 2001.

Long, Lynette. *Math Smarts: Tips, Tricks, and Secrets for Making Math More Fun!* Middleton, Wis.: American Girl, 2004.

Peterson, Ivars, and Nancy Peterson. *Math Trek: Adventures in the Math Zone.* New York: Jossey Bass, 1999.

Zaccaro, Edward. *The 10 Things All Future Mathematicians and Scientists Must Know (But Are Rarely Taught).* Bellevue, Iowa: Hickory Grove, 2003.

You can also try a little sleuthing around with some math mysteries at http://www.teacher.scholastic.com/maven/trail/index.htm.

🗣 WITH THE EXPERTS

American Mathematical Society
201 Charles Street
Providence, RI 02904-2294
http://www.ams.org

Association for Women in Mathematics
11240 Waples Mill Road, Suite 200
Fairfax, VA 22030-6078
http://www.awm-math.org

Mathematical Association of America
1529 18th Street NW
Washington, DC 20036-1358
http://www.maa.org

National Council of Teachers of Mathematics
1906 Association Drive
Reston, VA 20191-1502
http://www.nctm.org

Society for Industrial and Applied Mathematics
3600 University City Science Center, Suite 600
Philadelphia, PA 19104-2688
http://www.siam.org

GET ACQUAINTED

Lenore Blum, Mathematician

CAREER PATH

CHILDHOOD ASPIRATION: To be a mathematician.

FIRST JOB: Summer camp counselor.

CURRENT JOB: Distinguished career professor at Carnegie Mellon University where one of her highest priorities is to develop a model program for women in computer science.

A SMART COOKIE

Lenore Blum was born in New York City but moved with her family to Caracas, Venezuela, when she was still a young girl. This international experience provided some interesting educational and cultural experiences for Blum. It was in Caracas that she first discovered math as a fascinating, exciting subject waiting to be explored. Her love affair with math began with long division. She caught on to this concept instantly and kept learning all she could. Before long, she became known as the school's best student in math and graduated from high school when she was just 16.

When it came time to go to college, she initially followed a teacher's bad advice. She had wanted to major in mathematics, but the teacher told her that it was a "dead" field and that everything important had been discovered 2,000 years ago. Blum assumed that the only option was to blend mathematics with another subject in order to make it work, so Blum, also artistic and creative, decided to combine mathematics and art and pursue a degree in architecture.

By the second year of college, however, Blum was certain that mathematics was the way she wanted to go with her studies. Nothing challenged her as much or gave her as much satisfaction as figuring out complex mathematical formulas and truly understanding how all the pieces in the process fit together. She switched majors during her second year of college and has never regretted the decision.

DOING THE IMPOSSIBLE

Blum pursued her dream of becoming a mathematician at a time when women mathematicians were very rare. In fact, one of life's early disappointments came for Blum on the day she learned that she would not be admitted to the Massachusetts Institute of Technology (MIT), one of the best schools in mathematical sciences, to begin her college studies. It wasn't that she wasn't smart enough; the problem was her gender. Blum was a woman, and as one admissions officer told her, "MIT is no place for women." Princeton University, another prestigious school, did not even admit women until 1968—the same year that Blum earned her Ph.D.

The fact that Blum accomplished something that others thought couldn't or shouldn't be done says a great deal about her commitment to the profession. She had to overcome many obstacles to reach her professional goals and, in doing so, opened doors to greater opportunities for women in mathematics.

After distinguishing herself by hard work and dedication, Blum was eventually admitted to MIT to complete her graduate work. As it turned out, MIT was a place for this woman after all.

A CAREER THAT COUNTS

Blum's career officially began as a lecturer at the University of California at Berkeley in one of the best mathematics departments in the country. She worked there for two years and then was told she wouldn't be rehired. This was during the late 1960s when high-level opportunities for women in math were few and far between.

Blum realized that this situation would not change unless someone did something, so she joined a group of colleagues in forming the Association for Women in Mathematics. It didn't take long for her to build a reputation as an expert on women and mathematics.

Later she was hired to teach an algebra class at Mills College, an all-women's school. The course she was supposed to teach was so dull that she carefully designed a new one to introduce math as a link to new opportunities for young women. Her success in this effort led to a promotion as the head of a brand-new math and computer science department at the college.

BACK TO THE DRAWING BOARD

Eventually, Blum decided to devote all her professional energies to mathematical research. Her early work as a researcher focused on model theory, and she is credited with formulating new methods of logic to solve old problems in algebra. She has also worked with her husband, Manuel, to design computers that can learn the same way that small children do—by examples.

Blum is fascinated by why some problems seem to be hard and others not. This study is part of a new branch of mathematics and computer science called *complexity theory*. Complexity theory is important for cryptography (sending secret messages) and security (protecting your bank account) as well as for figuring out the best routes for sending messages over the Internet and shipping packages by UPS and Federal Express.

You can get an idea of Blum's work in complexity theory just by reading the titles of some of her published work:

On a Theory of Computation Over the Real Numbers: NP Completeness, Recursive Functions and Universal Machines; Towards an Asymptotic Analysis of Karmarkar's Algorithm; and Complexity and Real Computation. Don't let these technical titles scare you away from mathematics. Blum says this type of work is what she presents to fellow mathematicians. She also puts a lot of effort into making sure that everyday people can understand (and get excited about) mathematics.

A WORLD OF MATH

Blum's work has left its mark in places all over the world. She has made presentations at conferences throughout the United States and in Europe, China, Japan, Southeast Asia, the former Soviet Union, Latin America, and Africa. At the 1991 Pan-American Congress of Mathematicians, Blum represented the American Mathematical Society. The conference was held in Nairobi, Kenya, that year and made such an impression on Blum that she was inspired to start building links between the North American and African mathematics communities. Since then she has worked hard to construct an electronic communications link between the two continents.

According to Blum, jet-setting around the world is one of the hidden benefits of becoming a mathematician. With math, there are no borders between countries, and everyone speaks almost the same language. She sees the chance that math provides for people of different nationalities to work together on common problems as an important key to world peace.

A CHAMPION FOR THE CAUSE

Blum is especially well known for her efforts to get more girls involved in math and scientific fields. Aside from being a founding member of the Association for Women in Mathematics, she served as its president for several years. In addition, she helped create the Math/Science Network, which sponsors Expanding Your Horizons conferences around the country in order to get girls interested in math and science. Blum is credited for encouraging many young women to consider careers in math-intensive fields. She was recently honored for this work at the White House with the Presidential Award in Science, Mathematics, and Engineering.

Throughout her career, Blum has served as a role model for women in math. She's even earned such distinctions as becoming the first female editor of the prestigious *International Journal of Algebra and Computation* and being elected vice president of the American Mathematical Society. Suffice it to say that the success she's enjoyed during her career is worthy of emulation by mathematical minds of both genders.

You can read more about Blum's career in *Women and Numbers: Lives of Women Mathematicians* by Teri Perl (San Carlos, Calif.: Wide World, 1997).

Publisher

SKILL SET

✔ WRITING

✔ TALKING

✔ MONEY

WHAT IS A PUBLISHER?

It all started with the invention of moveable type by Johannes Gutenberg and his publication of the Bible in the mid-1400s. Since then, the publishing industry has blossomed to include all kinds of mediums—books, magazines, newspapers, CD-ROMs, and even electronic publishing. And behind all these words are publishers, who make it all happen.

In a traditional sense, a publisher is the biggest boss in a publishing company. He or she is ultimately responsible for deciding the overall direction the company will take. This means that the publisher decides if the company will specialize in children's books or sports books, a magazine for new parents, or whatever. Once the company's niche is established, the publisher generally has the final say in what books or other products are produced for each publishing season (publishers typically release new products in fall and spring catalogs). Maybe the most important responsibility that many publishers assume is putting up the money that it takes to acquire, print, market, and distribute the products published by their company. The old adage that you have to spend money in order to make money is certainly true for publishers.

With roughly 120,000 new books published each year, thousands of magazines published on a regular basis, and a wide variety of daily and weekly newspapers in operation, there is plenty of opportunity for people looking to make a living with words. However, you won't be walking out of high school or college and land the top spot in a publishing house. Not a chance. You are much more likely to work your way up through the ranks in the editorial, marketing, sales, or production departments of a publishing company. Working toward that top job is a goal worth pursuing and something to be proud of once you make it.

There are some interesting things happening in this industry that may have an impact on your future career in publishing. First is the way that a handful of publishers have

swallowed up a big chunk of the smaller houses to become megapublishers. They are so big, in fact, that it is estimated that just six of these big publishers capture about 60 percent of revenues earned on adult books. Second is a growing trend among entrepreneurial authors and publishers to buck the traditional publishing system and "do it their way." They are generally known as "self-publishers."

According to self-publishing experts Tom and Marilyn Ross, self-publishers "are sometimes called private publishers, independent publishers, small presses, or alternative publishers. But whatever label they may wear, they are, in a word, "mavericks," and they are part of a larger whole known as the small press movement—which, by the way, is growing at a breathtaking rate and has achieved not only respectability but extraordinary results."

Self-publishers are often authors who decide to publish their own work. Sometimes they tap into a specific niche such as crafts or health and publish a variety of related titles. The Internet is, of course, bringing new opportunities for innovative self-publishers too. Although it's almost impossible to keep track of how many self-publishers are at work, some say that there may well be as many as 55,000. Some are wildly successful and sell lots of books. Others are making a decent living, while others are losing money. E-books and online publishing opportunities are adding new and, some think, very promising ingredients to the mix.

Like traditional publishers, the self-publishers who are making a big splash have two things in common. First, they publish books that other people want to read. It seems pretty obvious, but one of most common mistakes publishers make is writing or publishing books that they want to write or read. Successful publishers of all sizes must first and foremost answer this question: Who wants to read this book?

Besides publishing quality books, all successful publishers also know how to sell their books. It's been said that bookstores are one of the worst places to sell a book. You can't expect to put a book in a store with thousands of other books and expect yours to fly off the shelf. Instead, publishers have to create a demand for their books. They do this through marketing, publicity, and specially crafted sales strategies. It's the only way to win the publishing game.

So what should you do if you want a future in books? Suggestion number one: read everything you can get your hands on—books, magazines, newspapers, even Web sites. Just read! Suggestion number two: Consider pursuing a degree in English, literature, journalism, or marketing to get your foot in the door of the profession. Suggestion number three: Get some experience with an established publisher. Try working in different departments to get a good look at all aspects of the publishing process. If your ultimate ambition is to someday start your own publishing company or to run an established house, do what you can to build your business skills. Some of the activities that follow will help you get started.

👉 TRY IT OUT

THE BEST OF THE BEST

Books are big business. Americans spend billions of dollars on books every year. A nice chunk of this income came from sales of books found on best-seller lists. The *New York Times* publishes one of the most famous best-seller lists every Sunday, and publishers everywhere want to land a book on that list. Find out what books are making it big this week by checking out the list online at http://www.nytimes.com/pages/books/bestseller. You may also want to see what major booksellers such as Barnes and Noble and Amazon.com have to say about the publishing superstars. You can find their lists at http://www.bn.com and http://www.amazon.com.

While you're at it, make up your own version of a "best-seller" list. Number a sheet of paper from 1 to 10, and list your all-time favorite books with the best one at the top of the list. Do any of the books on your list match the ones on the best-seller lists you found in the paper or on the Internet?

IN GOOD COMPANY

What do Huckleberry Finn, Tarzan, and the C-A-N-D-Y Monster all have in common? They were originally characters in self-published books by their respective authors: Mark Twain, Edgar Rice Burroughs, and Vicki Lansky.

Now it's your turn. If you want to find out what it's like to publish a book, just do it. Think of a really good idea that people in your "world" might buy. Maybe it's a directory of after-school activities or fun summer programs. How about a cookbook full of favorite recipes from kids and teachers at your school? Think of a good idea and make sure to ask yourself that all-important question: who would want to read a book like this? Possible customers might be other kids in your class, the school PTA, relatives, neighbors, libraries in your community, and so on.

✔ CHECK IT OUT

🖱 ON THE WEB
GET PUBLISHED!

If your plan is to someday publish other people's writing, you might want to get yourself published first. Right now. There are plenty of opportunities for kids just like you to see their writing in print. The Internet is one place to share your best work. Here are some Web sites where you can submit your writing and read the writing of other kids from all over the world:

- 💡 MidLink Magazine offers cyberspace for students to share their very best writing at http://www.cs.ucf.edu/MidLink.
- 💡 KidLit is another Web site that features literature and art produced by kids of various ages at http://www.mgfx.com/kidlit.
- 💡 KidPub is an award-winning Web site featuring more than 40,000 stories written by kids from all over the planet at http://www.kidpub.org.
- 💡 Try your writing skills, share your imagination, read fun stories, and maybe even get published on the Internet at http://www.kidscom.com/create/write/write.html.

- Investigate Cyberkids, an online magazine by kids and for kids at http://www.cyberkids.com.
- Submit your best work to *Stone Soup* magazine, a magazine by young writers and artists at http://www.stonesoup.com.

THE WRITE STUFF

Publishers learn to recognize good writing by writing themselves. Improve your own writing skills and enjoy some of these activities:

- Climb aboard an international storytelling train at http://storytrain.kids-space.org.
- Join the club at the Young Writer's Clubhouse at http://www.realkids.com/club.shtml.
- See what you can learn at the Young Writer's Workshop at http://www.planet.eon.net/bplaroch/index.html.
- Browse through the young writer's webzine at http://www.thescriptorium.net/youth.html.

And don't overlook writing opportunities that may be right under your nose. Your school, for instance, may have a student newspaper in need of budding writers like yourself. Ask around, and if there isn't one, talk to a teacher about helping you start one.

WHO WROTE IT?

Write a mystery! is a really fun site for mystery lovers. Investigate this very popular publishing genre and write your own mystery in the process. The Web site is http://www.thecase.com.

AT THE LIBRARY
READING ABOUT WRITING

Read all about how to be a good writer (keep pen and paper handy!) in the following books for young writers:

Allen, Susan, and Jane Lundman. *Written Anything Good Lately?* Minneapolis: Lerner, 2006.

Madden Kerry: *Writing Smarts: A Girl's Guide to Great Poetry, Stories, School Reports, and More.* Middleton, Wis.: Pleasant, 2002.

Nixon, Joan Lowery. *The Making of a Writer.* New York: Dell Yearling, 2003.

Olien, Rebecca. *Kids Write! Fantasy, Sci Fi, Autobiography, Adventure, and More.* Nashville, Tenn.: Ideals, 2006.

Rhatigan, Joe, and Veronika Gunter. *Write Now: The Ultimate Grab-a-Pen, Get-the-Words-Right, Have-a-Blast Writing Book.* New York: Sterling, 2005.

Scieszka, Jon. *Guys Write for Guys Read.* New York: Viking Penguin, 2005.

WITH THE EXPERTS

American Society of Magazine Editors
810 Seventh Avenue, 24 Floor
New York, NY 10019-5818
http://www.magazine.org/Editorial

Association of American Publishers
71 Fifth Avenue
New York, NY 10003-3004
http://www.publishers.org

Audio Publishers Association
8405 Greensboro Drive
McLean, VA 22102
http://www.audiopub.org

Magazine Publishers of America
810 Seventh Avenue, 24 Floor
New York, NY 10019-5818
http://www.magazine.org

National Newspaper Association
PO Box 7540
Columbia, MO 65205-7540
http://www.nna.org

Publishers Marketing Association
627 Aviation Way
Manhattan Beach, CA 90266-7107
http://www.pma-online.org

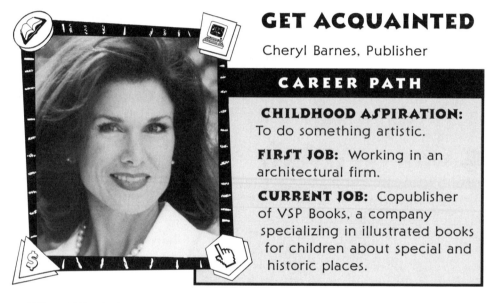

GET ACQUAINTED

Cheryl Barnes, Publisher

CAREER PATH

CHILDHOOD ASPIRATION:
To do something artistic.

FIRST JOB: Working in an architectural firm.

CURRENT JOB: Copublisher of VSP Books, a company specializing in illustrated books for children about special and historic places.

THE DYNAMIC DUO

As copublisher along with her husband Peter, Cheryl Shaw Barnes wears a lot of hats. She helps write the books, she often illustrates them, she visits schools to talk about her books, she goes to bookstores to sign her books, she does everything she can think of to sell more books, and until recently she even packed the books up to send to customers. That's the way it goes for an independent publisher, but, according to the Barneses, it is worth it.

Their company, VSP Books, has published more than 25 books and a couple of teacher's guides. By publishing the books themselves, the Barneses estimate that they earn 300 to 400 percent more than they would if they let someone else publish their books for them.

They like the extra income as well as the control they have over their books. Doing everything themselves allows them to give each title the same tender loving care they would give to a new baby—well, almost. At the very least, they can be sure that the books are produced with the quality their reputation rests on and that the books get the best of all chances to find their way into the hands of young readers.

THE WEIRDEST THING HAPPENED

VSP Books came about in an unusual way. Barnes and her husband were vacationing one summer on Nantucket Island in Massachusetts when they overheard someone ask a gift shop owner for a children's book about the island. The owner told them there wasn't one. The idea for a publishing company was born, and their first book launched soon afterward. The book, *Nat, Nat, the Nantucket Cat*, continues to sell several thousand copies each year in just a handful of shops frequented by tourists.

It's a formula that has worked for other "destination" books as well, including *Alexander the Old Town Mouse* about historic Alexandria, Virginia; *Martha's Vineyard* about the scenic island in Massachusetts; and *Cornelius Vandermouse, the Pride of Newport*, about historic Newport, Rhode Island.

If the publishing company itself came about in an unusual way, the Barneses' turn toward publishing books about the government came about in a really strange way. One afternoon, Barnes was enjoying watching one of her daughters play lacrosse when a woman, the mother of another player, came stomping across the field toward her. The woman, who had worked in the administrations of Presidents George Bush and Ronald Reagan, told Barnes, "I know what book you're going to do next." Barnes thought that was rather odd since she didn't even know what book she was going to do next, but the woman seemed fairly certain. It turns out that part of the woman's job involved choosing gifts for foreign dignitaries and their families. She had decided that she was tired of giving fake handcuffs from the FBI to the children of these visitors, and she wanted a book about the White House to give instead. Impressed with the quality of Barnes's previous books, the woman thought that Barnes was the right choice to create a delightful book about the "people's" house.

Before Barnes knew it, she was off to the White House with a fancy camera to take pictures of every nook and cranny. She used the pictures to illustrate *Woodrow, the White House Mouse*, the book she and her husband wove around the presidency and America's most famous house.

One thing led to another after that. Someone from the Capitol called and wanted a book about Congress. The result was *House Mouse, Senate Mouse*. They couldn't leave out the third branch of the federal government, so *Marshall, the Courthouse Mouse* was soon to follow. One of their latest books, *Woodrow for President*, explains the electoral process in an easy-to-understand and hard-to-forget way.

YOU KNOW YOU'VE MADE IT WHEN . . .

An episode of *The Rosie O'Donnell Show* proved that Barnes was doing a good job getting the word out about their books. One day Barnes was sitting in her home office signing books, packing orders, and half paying attention to Rosie's show when one of her assistants pointed to the television. There on the show a very important guest was giving a copy of *Woodrow, the White House Mouse* as a gift to Rosie's son. The guest was none other than former First Lady Hillary Clinton. It was a nice surprise and a wonderful bit of free publicity for Barnes's books.

THE LITTLE ENGINE THAT COULD

When Barnes was a child, her favorite book was *The Little Engine That Could*. She could relate to that plucky little engine that worked so hard to get up the hill. That's because Barnes is dyslexic, and she had a really hard time learning to read. In fact, she didn't learn how to read until she was in the third grade. It was a hard thing to deal with because all the other kids could already read. Fortunately, she had some good teachers who helped her build up her confidence while her brain was working hard to catch up with the other kids.

One teacher in particular helped her discover her very special abilities as an artist.

Barnes says her learning disability turned out to be a good thing in her life. It made her work harder and gave her a strength she wouldn't have otherwise had—traits that come in handy as she continues to create wonderful books and build a publishing business.

P.S.

You can find out more about Barnes and her books at http://www.vspbooks.com.

Real Estate Agent

WHAT IS A REAL ESTATE AGENT?

A real estate agent knows property—where it is, how much it's worth, and how to buy or sell it. An agent may specialize in residential property (places where people live), commercial property (places where people work), or resort property (places where people play). Some agents do business in a particular community or city, while others cover a broader geographic region or specific type of property. Still others work internationally and handle property transactions in a certain part of the world such as a European country or in resort areas such as the Caribbean.

Whether they deal with condominiums or skyscrapers, most realtors work both sides of the "game"—they either work with people who want to buy property or those who want to sell it. Either way, the challenge is to find the right match—the perfect place for someone to buy or the perfect person to buy a place. To do this successfully, real estate agents must know a lot about both property and people. They must be knowledgeable about things such as zoning laws, mortgage rates, financing options, tax rates, and insurance coverage. They must be able to listen to what their clients say about what they are looking for (which sometimes means reading between the lines) and find homes or business properties that meet their needs and budgets.

Even the most basic real estate transactions tend to be fairly complicated. Just selling or buying a house can involve piles of paperwork. There are contracts, deeds, disclosures, financial statements, and all kinds of other legal documents. Computers play an important part in helping real estate professionals manage the paperwork, and they help agents keep track of market trends and available properties.

Agents also use computers to conduct region-wide or even worldwide searches for property that matches a client's criteria. Clients tell an agent exactly what they want; the agent clicks a few buttons and out comes a list of properties that match the clients' needs. Talk about the ultimate in matchmaking! You can also take a "virtual tour" of a property online and see inside a house thousands of miles away.

While being an agent is probably the first career that comes to mind when you think of real estate, there are actually many interesting professions related to the sale, management, and analysis of property.

Appraisers investigate the quality of a given piece of property to determine its value. They do this by gathering information about the property, taking measurements, interviewing people familiar with the property's history, and searching public records of sales, leases, and other transactions. They also compare the property with other similar properties to come up with a fair estimate of the property's value. Appraisers compile their findings into a report for a bank or other type of financial lending institution. A bank will not loan money on a property unless its appraised value meets or exceeds the loan amount, so this process is important to buyers and sellers alike.

Loan officers are the "money" people who typically work for banks or mortgage companies and help arrange financing for people or businesses who are purchasing property.

Property developers are entrepreneurs who buy land and turn it into neighborhoods, resorts, or office complexes. A good property developer can look at an empty field and see a bustling community. It takes vision, an ability to manage big projects, a knowledge of building and construction techniques, and money—lots of it.

Property managers take care of other people's or companies' real estate investments. They might manage any number of residential homes, apartments or condominiums, office buildings, retail stores, or industrial properties. Their duties typically include handling the financial dealings of the property—paying bills and taxes and collecting rents. They may also handle all the day-to-day matters involved in keeping a property clean and well cared for. Property managers or management companies are paid by the owners of the property.

While some people go into real estate or appraising with little more than a high school diploma, others have college degrees in areas such as business, management, or real estate management. But no one goes into real estate or appraising without the proper certification. Certification usually involves passing a test and other requirements by a professional organization such as the National Association of Realtors.

Success in any career in real estate tends to hinge on a couple of common traits. One trait is an entrepreneurial spirit. Many real estate careers offer unique opportunities to do your own thing and be your own boss. In fact, it is the flexible nature of the work that draws many people to the profession. Essentially, real estate agents work as hard as they want to work, choose how many (or how few) hours they want to devote to their work, and reap the results accordingly. Obviously, the harder (and the smarter) they work, the more income they earn.

Experience is another common trait. It takes time to build up a client base and to learn the ropes in real estate. You can expect to find lots of experience—and a little luck—behind the most successful people in this business.

Maybe the most important trait of a real estate agent is the ability to "close the deal." This involves negotiating with clients to work out arrangements that suit everyone. It takes people skills and communication skills, and you won't make it far in this profession without them.

☞ TRY IT OUT

REAL ESTATE HOMEWORK

The local school system is one thing that many families consider when looking for a new home. What if you were trying to sell a home in your neighborhood? What could you tell your client about the nearby schools?

Make a list of the preschools, elementary schools, middle schools, and high schools that kids in your neighborhood attend. Find out any special features about each school to make a good "sales pitch." For instance, the elementary school has a brand-new computer center, the middle school has the highest test scores in the area, the high school has a winning football team—all the things people tend to brag about.

For some official information, see what you can find about these schools at The School Report (http://www.

homefair.com/SR_home.html), a Web site offering nation-wide statistics on schools and frequently used by real estate professionals. Gathering this type of information is called market research and would be an important part of a career in real estate.

REAL ESTATE MATCHMAKING

Matching people with properties is, in a nutshell, what the real estate business is all about. Give your matchmaking skills a workout with the following activity. First, gather a couple of real estate magazines, the real estate classified advertising section from Sunday's newspaper, and any resources you can find that include pictures of houses and other types of buildings.

Now, read these client profiles carefully:

- Family of four, both parents work in the city, one child is in elementary school, the other child is a toddler. Need three or four bedrooms, at least two bathrooms, and an attached garage. Looking for a family-friendly neighborhood with good schools and child care options.
- Retired couple, wife is in a wheelchair, looking for nice, affordable, one-story home in a quiet area. New construction is desirable in order to easily accommodate wife's disability.
- New software business looking for 5,000 square feet of office space in downtown area or business park with easy access to major roads. A "build to suit" situation would be ideal.
- Single person in mid-20s, just landed a great new job, looking for a "cool" place to call home. Must have lots of amenities for active social life including clubhouse, pool, and workout facilities.

Designate a separate sheet of paper for each situation and attach pictures of homes and properties as well as classified advertisements that might interest each client.

✔ CHECK IT OUT

🖱 ON THE WEB
VIRTUAL TOURS

The Internet has opened new doors in real estate. For instance, if you live in Dallas and have just learned that your new job promotion means you'll have to relocate to Los Angeles, you can sit in front of your computer and find a new home on the Internet. At least that's how it works in theory. Most people still want to have an old-fashioned look at the actual property. But virtual tours of the property can save everyone a lot of time and effort. It's also a great way for you to learn more about the real estate business.

Use the following Web sites to compare the costs of a four- or five-bedroom luxury home in at least three different parts of the country:

- 💡 http://www.realestate.com
- 💡 http://www.homedebut.com
- 💡 http://www.360house.com

Print out pictures of the properties you find and make a chart showcasing where you can get the most house for the least money.

📚 AT THE LIBRARY
HOME, SWEET, WORLD

Be it ever so humble, there's no place like home. Whether it's an igloo or a mansion, a condo or a thatched hut, people the world over would agree with that statement. Take a look at the places the world calls home in books such as:

Adams, McCrea. *Tipi: Native American Home.* Vero Beach, Fla.: Rourke, 2003.
Hall, Margaret. *Around the World: Homes.* Portsmouth, N.H.: Heinemann, 2003.

Komatsu, Yoshio. *Wonderful Houses Around the World.* Bolinas, Calif.: Shelter, 2004.

MacDonald, Fiona. *Homes: Discovering World Cultures.* New York: Crabtree, 2001.

Mattern, Joanne. *Homes: Yesterday and Today.* Farmington Hills, Mich.: Blackbirch, 2004.

Spilsbury, Louise. *Moving People: Migration and Settlement.* Eustis, Fla.: Raintree, 2006.

Wirkner, Linda. *Learning About Urban Growth in America with Graphic Organizers.* New York: Powerkids, 2005.

WITH THE EXPERTS

Air Commercial Real Estate Association
800 West 6th Street, Suite 800
Los Angeles, CA 90017-2704
http://www.airea.com

American Real Estate and Urban Economics Association
PO Box 9958
Richmond, VA 23228-9958
http://www.areuea.org

National Association of Industrial and Office Properties
2201 Cooperative Way, 3rd Floor
Hendron, VA 20171-3034
http://www.naiop.org

National Association of Real Estate Brokers
9831 Greenbelt Road
Lanham, MD 20706-2202
http://www.nareb.com

National Association of Realtors
430 North Michigan Avenue
Chicago, IL 60611-4011
http://www.realtor.org

Society of Industrial and Office Realtors
1201 New York Avenue NW, Suite 350
Washington, DC 20005-6126
http://www.sior.com

GET ACQUAINTED

Nishat Karimi, Real Estate Agent

CAREER PATH

CHILDHOOD ASPIRATION:
Wanted to be a doctor until all the blood grossed her out.

FIRST JOB: Sales clerk at a boutique in a mall.

CURRENT JOB: President of Nishat Karimi Realty, LLC (http://www.nishatkarimirealty.com).

MIXING CAREERS AND REAL LIFE

Nishat Karimi graduated from college with a degree in business administration. She started her career working in marketing for the May Company and worked her way up to area sales manager before she and her husband decided to start a family. Although she really enjoyed the work, the job involved quite a bit of travel and long hours. So once the babies started coming, Karimi quit her job to take care of them.

As the children got older Karimi decided it was time to go back to work. However, she didn't want a job that would lock her into a full-time schedule. She wanted a job with flexible hours that she could do from home.

That's when Karimi found out about real estate. It looked like a good fit with her business and marketing background, and it would allow her to keep her home and work responsibilities more balanced. To get started, Karimi had to take special courses in real estate—one on the basics, another on contracts, and another in finance. Then she had to pass an exam in order to qualify for a real estate license.

Real Estate Agent

Even with a license, new agents have to work under a certified real estate broker, so Karimi signed up with a big, independent real estate company working in the Dallas/Forth Worth area. Even though she works for a big company, Karimi is in business for herself. No one tells her when and how long she has to work, and no one tells her what to do or how to run her business. Karimi decides all that for herself. But the company does provide things such as office space, a solid reputation, and other perks. They don't provide these things for free, of course, but the arrangement works out well for both Karimi and the real estate company.

FINDING A NICHE

Originally from Pakistan, Karimi speaks the Hindi language fluently. Karimi uses this skill to market her services to the many South Asian people relocating to Dallas. Because she knows the language and understands the customs of these home buyers, many of whom are in the United States for the first time, she is able to help them in ways other agents cannot. Her background provides a natural "in" with a growing segment of the metropolitan Dallas population and adds a very profitable international angle to her business. Karimi believes this edge is one reason why she recently was named "rookie of the year" at her company.

THE REAL STORY ABOUT REAL ESTATE

Karimi is quick to dispel the myth that all real estate agents are rich. Sure, making a lot of money is possible—and highly desirable. But it takes a lot of hard work and time to build up a good base of clients. Real estate agents have to get the word out that they are in business.

Having worked in the business for a couple years now, Karimi is still building that base and spends a good chunk of her time prospecting for clients—by sending out special mailings, hosting open houses, advertising on Hindi-language radio stations, and letting everyone she meets know that she is a realtor. She says that satisfied clients are really her best forms of advertising. If she does a good job for someone, that person will tell his or her friends and their friends will come to her when they need to buy or sell a house.

FEAST OR FAMINE

Real estate agents do not get a paycheck every week. Instead, they get a commission from each property that they sell (usually about 3 percent per agent for buyer and seller). This is good news and bad news. The good news is that when agents do sell a property, they can earn some pretty big bucks (upwards of $5,000 to $10,000 per sale). The bad news is: no sales, no pay. Karimi says that during certain parts of the year, such as spring and summer, things are so hectic that it's all she can do to keep up with the business. Other times, such as the winter months, she feels as though she spends a lot of time twiddling her thumbs. This part of her job makes Karimi especially glad that she has a background in business. She is careful to invest her earnings so that they stretch to cover the slow times.

Her business background also comes in handy when it comes to planning her business strategies. So far, Karimi's goal has been to double her sales every year, and so far she has done just that. At this pace, Karimi is well on her way to becoming a real estate superstar!

FYI

You can find out more about Karimi's work on her Web site at http://www.northdallasproperties.com.

Stockbroker

SHORTCUTS

SKILL SET

✔ BUSINESS

✔ ADVENTURE

✔ MATH

GO watch the daily financial news on a television station such as CNN or Fox News.

READ the *Wall Street Journal* (http://www.usj.com).

TRY picking a stock and tracking its ups and downs over several weeks.

WHAT IS A STOCKBROKER?

A stockbroker's job is to invest other people's money in the stock market. Whether it's an investment of a few hundred dollars or a few million, a stockbroker works with individual clients to develop an "investment portfolio" that best meets their financial goals. For instance, some people prefer investments that have the potential to earn a big return in a short amount of time. These risk-takers have to be carefully positioned to enjoy the gains yet sustain the inevitable losses that come with this type of investing. Other clients may prefer safe, steady investments that provide a profit over time.

To satisfy the needs of all kinds of clients, a stockbroker must know how the stock market works, must be extremely knowledgeable about all kinds of investments, and must stay current on the constantly changing financial status of a wide variety of investment options. In addition, a stockbroker must be able to convey all this information to clients in a way that wins their trust—and their investment capital.

Some stockbrokers work in an office managing their clients' investments, and some actually trade on the floor of the stock market. Either way, a stockbroker's work is fast paced and intense. Stockbrokers often have to think quickly, using both well-researched information and their own good instincts.

Stockbrokers spend a lot of time on the telephone and may talk with 50 to 100 clients each day. They also read

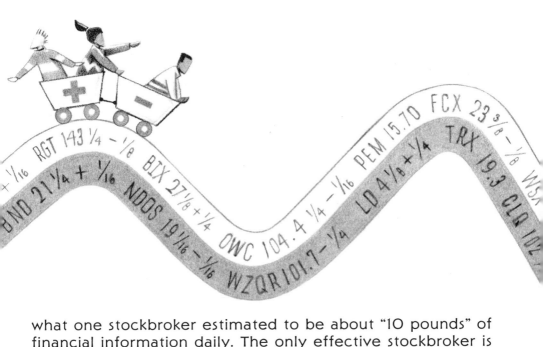

what one stockbroker estimated to be about "10 pounds" of financial information daily. The only effective stockbroker is an informed stockbroker. Yesterday's news is often not good enough in a profession where fortunes can be made and lost overnight.

Stockbrokers can work anywhere—in big cities and little towns. When they want to buy or sell stock for one of their customers, they have to place an order with a floor trader who works in a stock exchange. The New York Stock Exchange is the oldest and biggest exchange. There are also exchanges in San Francisco, Chicago, Boston, Cincinnati, and Philadelphia, as well as in different parts of the world.

In some ways, U.S. stock exchanges are much like they were a century ago. Traders still congregate in pits and make trades by yelling out offers. Deals worth millions of dollars are made by one trader negotiating a price with another trader. Their word is all it takes to close the sale.

In other ways, stock exchanges are a great example of the wonders of modern technology. Thousands of miles of communication lines link stockbrokers in offices all over the country to traders in exchanges worldwide. This high-tech arrangement allows a stockbroker in London to order stock from a floor trader in Los Angeles in a matter of minutes. In addition, cell phones and pagers have added to the break-neck speed and the efficiency of floor trading.

In order to trade on the floor of a stock exchange, floor traders must either belong to a firm that has a "seat" on the exchange or purchase one for themselves for $600,000. Of course, having a seat on the exchange is a bit misleading. Floor traders are generally on their feet all day, rushing from pit to pit making bids.

Becoming a stockbroker does not require a college degree, although most stockbrokers have one. It does require passing the General Securities Registered Representative Examination, which a person can take after being employed by a brokerage firm for at least four months. In some states stockbrokers also have to pass the Uniform Securities Agents State Law Examination. This process is meant to be a safe-guard to ensure that stockbrokers know what they are doing before they start dealing with other people's money.

☞ TRY IT OUT

BULL OR BEAR MARKET?

Is it a bull or bear market? Don't have a clue? Go online to the Investor Words Web site at http://www.investorwords. com and brush up on stock market terminology. While you're there you might as well start your own stock market diction-ary by looking up the following:

Bull market	High flyer
Bear market	Junk bond
Bid	Mutual fund
Black Monday	P/E ratio
Crash of 1927	Split

Record what you find in a small notebook or on index cards. As your knowledge of the stock market grows so should your pile of dictionary entries.

GO FOR THE GUSTO!

For those who can't decide which they like best—playing sports or making money—here's your chance to have it all. Use your computer to access SportShares Web site (http://www.sportshares.com). This free Internet game combines the excitement of fantasy sports with the challenge of the stock market by converting teams and players from the professional sports world into stocks that you buy and sell.

Your goal is to build and manage an account of fantasy shares that outperforms the competition in an effort to win fame and fortune. There are links to all your favorite professional sports teams, and you can take your pick of which game to play: fantasy baseball, basketball, football, golf, hockey, NASCAR, or soccer.

So, what are you waiting for? Pick a team, make a chart, and start tracking the winnings and earnings of your team.

 **CHECK IT OUT**

ON THE WEB

PLAY THE STOCK MARKET GAME

Every year thousands of students learn about the stock market at school playing virtual stock market games. Find out if your school or teacher wants to play either as part of a math or social studies unit or in an after-school club. Information about two of the most widely used online stock market simulation games can be found at these Web sites:

- The Stock Market Game at http://www.smg2000.org.
- National SMS: Stock Market Simulation Game at http://nationalsms.com.

Or to strike out on your own, ask your parents to help you get started at any of these Web sites:

- 💡 SimuStock at http://www.simustock.com/
- 💡 Stock Market Quest at http://www.stockmarket-quest.com
- 💡 Young Money at http://www.youngmoney.com/stock_market_game

SMART MONEY ONLINE

Find out more about money, investing, and all things financial online.

- 💡 Go for the big money at http://www.agedwards.com/public/content/fcgi/bma/bma.fcgi.
- 💡 Find an introduction to investing at http://www.pbs.org/newshour/on2/money/stocks.html.
- 💡 Get advice for young fools by http://www.fool.com/teens/teens.htm.

📚 AT THE LIBRARY

READ YOUR WAY INTO THE INSIDE TRACK

For a good basic introduction to how the stock market works, read some of the following books:

Condon, Daniel. *Playing the Market: Stocks and Bond.* Portsmouth, N.H.: Heinemann, 2003.

Fuller, Donna Jo. *The Stock Market: How Economics Works.* Minneapolis: Lerner, 2005.

McGowan, Eileen. *Stock Market Smart.* Minneapolis: Millbrook, 2002.

You may also want to read up on one of Wall Street's worst times in books such as:

Blumenthal, Karen. *Six Days in October: The Stock Market Crash of 1929.* New York: Atheneum, 2002.

Woolf, Alex. *The Wall Street Crash, October 29, 1929.* Chicago: Raintree, 2002.

✒️ WITH THE EXPERTS

American Financial Services Association
919 18th Street NW, Suite 300
Washington, DC 20006-5517
http://www.afsaonline.org/sitepages/1.cfm

American Stock Exchange
86 Trinity Place
New York, NY 10006-1818
http://www.amex.com

CFA Institute
560 Ray C. Hunt Drive
Charlottesville, VA 22903-2981
http://www.cfainstitute.org

Chicago Board of Options Exchange
400 South La Salle Street
Chicago, IL 60605-1023
http://www.cboe.com

New York Stock Exchange
11 Wall Street
New York, NY 10005-1905
http://www.nyse.com

Pacific Stock Exchange
115 Sansome Street
San Francisco, CA 94104-3601
http://www.pacificex.com

Philadelphia Stock Exchange
1900 Market Street
Philadelphia, PA 19103-3527
http://www.phlx.com

Securities Industry Association
120 Broadway, 35th Floor
New York, NY 10271-0080
http://www.sia.com

GET ACQUAINTED

Jim Cramer, Stockbroker

CAREER PATH

FIRST JOB: Selling ice cream at Veterans Stadium during Philadelphia Phillies games.

CURRENT POSITION: Host of the very successful *Mad Money* television show.

NEVER TOO EARLY TO START

They call him the Mad Man of Wall Street. Thanks to his wildly popular and rambunctious television show, *Mad Money*, Jim Cramer is probably one of the most famous Wall Street investors ever. Most people know that he's smart, successful, and savvy about the stock market. What they don't know is that he started learning about the stock market when he was just nine years old!

His interest in stocks followed him to Harvard University where, as editor of the school's newspaper the *Harvard Crimson*, he learned how to express his ideas and opinions in such a way that other people listened to what he had to say. In one case, an article he wrote made one of his professors so angry that he refused to give Cramer his diploma during the commencement ceremonies. The public snub was so upsetting to Cramer's parents that he says they didn't stop crying all the way home. The professor and the school later apologized, but the incident proved an interesting start to a career built around speaking his own mind.

TWO INTERESTS, ONE GREAT CAREER

After working for a couple years for the *Los Angeles Herald Examiner*, Cramer returned to Harvard to earn a law degree.

He worked for a couple years in the trading department at Goldman Sachs before starting his own hedge fund. Within a short time the company Cramer and his partner started was earning better returns than some of the biggest and best firms on Wall Street.

After proving himself as a trading force to be reckoned with, Cramer decided to blend his two passions—investing and journalism—by cofounding a financial news Web site called TheStreet.com (http://www.thestreet.com).

Cramer's career has taken off from there. He's written books, he hosts a radio talk show, and he even stars in his very own television show. Along the way, since he also practices his own advice on investing, he's made a lot of money.

KID-SIZED ADVICE FROM CRAMER

If you were to ask Jim Cramer how to get rich trading stocks, he's likely to suggest some very familiar advice: Do your homework. That's what he often advises his viewers on *Mad Money*, and it's a strategy that certainly seems to be working for him. He knows so much about so many publicly traded companies that it is nothing short of absolutely amazing. His is a classic example of practicing what he preaches. Before he invests his (or anyone else's) money he learns as much as he can about a company's performance and has learned to predict with astounding accuracy which companies are headed for big time success and which ones are headed for trouble. As Cramer is fond of saying with great gusto, "Booyah!"

STAY IN TOUCH WITH CRAMER

There are lots of ways you can find out more about Jim Cramer, his work, and his ideas about the stock market. You could read his book—*Jim Cramer's Real Money: Sane Investing in an Insane World* (New York: Simon and Schuster, 2005). You could watch his show *Mad Money* every day Monday through Friday at 6:00 P.M. or 9:00 P.M. on the CNBC channel, or you might listen to his *Real Money with Jim Cramer* radio show online anytime at http://www.thestreet.com/m/radio.

Urban Planner

WHAT IS AN URBAN PLANNER?

An urban planner works with one goal in mind: to make life better for people. An urban planner does this by creating environments that are functional, comfortable, convenient, healthy, efficient, and attractive. He or she must promote the best use of a community's land and resources for places where people live, work, and play. Whether designing a beautiful park, curbing traffic congestion, or combating pollution, the urban planner applies creative solutions to complex problems that affect people and the world around them.

Urban planners work to make improvements that will meet the needs of people and their communities now and in the years to come. Their work may involve a single building, a neighborhood, a small town, a city, a county, or a metropolitan region. Sometimes they may be designing an entire city or neighborhood from scratch. Other times their work involves preserving historical landmarks or redeveloping decaying areas such as those in the older sections of a large city.

Regardless of the type of project, the single most important skill for urban planners is the ability to see the big picture. They must be able to capture a vision of all that a given project might involve and how it connects to all other aspects of a community. The next most important skill for planners is the ability to convey that vision to others in pictures and in words. To complete the picture part, most planners find that a blend of artistic creativity and computer savvy allows them to illustrate and define their project so others can understand their ideas. Sharing their ideas in words requires excellent writing and speaking skills. Because the nature of their work often represents change and people tend to resist change, planners must present their ideas using diplomatic and persuasive communication skills.

Planners are often employed by government agencies of all sizes on a city, county, state, or federal level. They are also employed by architectural firms, engineering firms, and real-estate development companies. Depending on the nature of their responsibilities, planners may specialize in areas such as environmental planning, land-use planning, and water resource management. Their work often requires them to interface with architects, engineers, construction contractors, and other professionals who turn a planner's ideas into reality.

A college degree in urban planning, civil engineering, architecture, or public administration is required to get a job as an urban planner. Some planners find that a master's degree in a field such as structural engineering may become necessary if they wish to advance in their career.

Those who are interested in this type of work but prefer less training might consider related jobs such as surveyor, drafter, computer-aided design (CAD) specialist, or landscaper. The common thread that links these professions with urban planning is a desire to use creative skills to make the world a better and more beautiful place.

☞ TRY IT OUT

KID TOWN, U.S.A.

Here's your chance to have things your way. Close your eyes and imagine a place where everything is geared for people just your age. The activities, the buildings, the stores, the modes of transportation—everything. Let your imagination go wild and focus on the details. Now, grab a notebook and pen, and make a list of all the special features of your wanna-be, wish-it-could-be town. Use your ideas to create a poster or sketch so that others can share your vision for a town that's just right for kids like you.

Go a step further and build a model of your town using boxes. For complete instructions and lots of stretch-the-imagination planning activities, use Ginny and Dean Graves's fun resource entitled *Box City: An Interdisciplinary Experience in Community Planning* (Prairie Village, Kans.: Center for Understanding the Built Environment, 1999), or go online to http://www.cubekc.org for more information.

READING BETWEEN THE BUILDINGS

The Center for Understanding the Built Environment (CUBE) is an organization that encourages young people to work together to create a quality-built and natural environment. Visit CUBE's Web site at http://www.cubekc.org, where you'll find ideas for many activities including Reading a Building. This activity gives you a new look at familiar buildings, encouraging you to really notice details such as the walls, the roof, the windows, and the doors as well as special features such as arches, columns, and other ornaments.

You can use the chart found at http://www.cubekc.org/architivities/rab.html to record your discoveries. As you observe the structure, remember that each of those features is a result of planning and design. See if you can get inside the designer's head and draw some conclusions about why certain choices were made. How do all those elements come together to create a building that is well used and well loved?

MY TOWN IS BEST

For the sake of this activity, let's assume that you really like the place where you live. Suppose your job was to design a postcard enticing other people your age to visit your town. Start by spelling out the name of your town in big, fancy letters. Use each of the letters to illustrate or describe something that makes your town special. Feel free to use a computer program to help with the graphics. Just do everything you can to make it inviting and eye-catching.

For additional information and ideas, visit another one of CUBE's activity pages at http://www.cubekc.org/architivities/postcard.html.

✔ CHECK IT OUT

🖱 ON THE WEB

BUILD IT AND THEY WILL COME

If virtual reality is more your thing, you can create and run your own amazing city on the scale of San Francisco or Berlin with *Sim City 4000*, a computer software game published by Electronic Arts. You can find this game at most major toy or software stores or order it online at http://www.simcity.ea.com.

A STROLL AROUND THE INTERNET

Wander around some of these Web sites of interest to future urban planners:

☼ Discover architecture through the ages at http:// library.thinkquest.org/10098.

☼ Enjoy some arch*kid*ecture at http://www.arch kidecture.org.

☼ Build your own roller coaster at http://kids.discovery. com/games/rollercoasters/buildacoaster.html.

☼ Explore architecture for kids at http://www.ebuilding connections.com.

☼ Get the inside story on those ancient Egyptian pyramids at http://www.pbs.org/wgbh/nova/pyramid.

☼ Check out a site for kids that was developed by America's city planners at http://www.planning. org/KidsAndCommunity.

AT THE LIBRARY
URBAN PLANNING 101

The following books will start you on your quest for knowledge about urban planning:

Englar, Mary. *I. M. Pei (Asian American Biographies)*. Chicago: Raintree, 2005.

Millard, Anne. *A Street Through Time*. New York: DK, 2004.

Oxlade, Chris. *Bridges: Building Amazing Structures*. Portsmouth, N.H.: Heinemann, 2005.

———. *Canals: Building Amazing Structures*. Portsmouth, N.H.: Heinemann, 2005.

———. *Skyscrapers: Uncovering Technology*. New York: Firefly Books, 2006.

Sullivan, George. *Built to Last*. New York: Scholastic, 2005.

WELCOME TO WALTOPIA

If anyone ever had grand plans for great cities, it was Walt Disney. Creator of Mickey Mouse and founder of the Disneyland and Walt Disney World entertainment empire, this man dared to dream big dreams and, even better, had the courage to make them happen. Epcot, another part of the Disney entertainment empire, began as Walt Disney's dream of a perfect city. You can get a look at Disney's original plans, as well as photographs of the result of that dream, at an award-winning Web site called Waltopia. Find it at http://www.waltopia.com.

◖ WITH THE EXPERTS

American Institute of Architects
1735 New York Avenue NW
Washington, DC 20006-5292
http://www.aia.org

American Institute of Certified Planners
1776 Massachusetts Avenue NW
Washington, DC 20036-1904
http://www.planning.org

American Planning Association
122 South Michigan Avenue, Suite 1600
Chicago, IL 60603-6191
http://www.planning.org

Center for Understanding the Built Environment (CUBE)
5328 West 67th Street
Prarie Village, KS 66208-1408
http://www.cubekc.org

Planning and Design Institute
241 North Broadway
Milwaukee, WI 53202-5819
http://www.pdisite.com

Urban Land Institute
1025 Thomas Jefferson Street NW, Suite 500 West
Washington, DC 20007-5224
http://www.uli.org

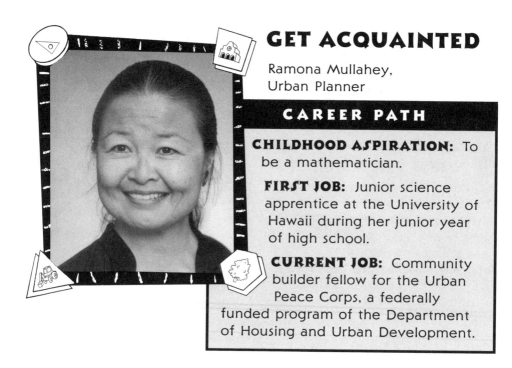

GET ACQUAINTED

Ramona Mullahey,
Urban Planner

CAREER PATH

CHILDHOOD ASPIRATION: To be a mathematician.

FIRST JOB: Junior science apprentice at the University of Hawaii during her junior year of high school.

CURRENT JOB: Community builder fellow for the Urban Peace Corps, a federally funded program of the Department of Housing and Urban Development.

IT DIDN'T ADD UP

Ramona Mullahey was named after her aunt, a math teacher. Wanting to live up to the honor of her name, Mullahey took all the math classes she could in high school and went to college with the intention of following in her aunt's footsteps as a mathematician. On the way to getting her degree, she discovered something important. Math wasn't the right choice for her. Sure, she liked math and she was good at it, but there was another side to her that didn't want there to be just one right answer all the time.

She ended up switching to a political science major, which is often used as a stepping stone for law school. But in order to get into law school, you have to pass a really tough exam. Mullahey took the exam and flunked it—twice. So much for that idea.

Although the experience was unpleasant, it reinforced the idea that Mullahey just wasn't cut out for work that required her to fit all the answers into a neat little box. She worked best when she could be creative and find different ways to solve problems and use information.

THIS IS IT!

Mullahey found the perfect fit when she was thumbing through a college catalog. The college offered programs in planning and architecture. Working with people to shape communities was one of the ways the catalog described the careers associated with the degrees. That concept clicked with Mullahey in a big way. She says it completely resonated with who she was and what she wanted to do with her life. She decided to go for it and has never looked back.

ALOHA COMMUNITIES

Mullahey was born and raised in Hawaii. She says that one of the most satisfying parts of her work as a planner has involved historic and cultural preservation projects. While the work is important for honoring the traditions of the past, it also helps give people a sense of who they are and a respect for where they are. For this reason, one project in particular was especially rewarding for Mullahey.

This project involved cleaning and restoring the site of a heiau, a native Hawaiian religious place. Originally the site had been considered sacred and was marked by monuments made of stone. When Mullahey and her team came on the scene, the site was overwhelmed by trash and overgrown with weeds. It was no small task returning the site back to a place of distinction. Mullahey relied on a group of hardworking partners from government, business, the nonprofit sector, and the community to do the dirty work. Their efforts paid off when the project was honored with an award from the National Trust for Historic Preservation.

CREATING A NEW TOWN

Another big project that Mullahey has worked on involved transforming what had long been a rural sugarcane town on the island of Oahu into a thriving suburban city. The project has an eventual goal of providing affordable and market housing for 120,000 people. It involves building neighborhoods, schools, businesses, shopping malls, and all the other places that mark a small city.

Mullahey's involvement in this project included three phases. Her first task was to educate the existing community about what planning is all about and what the new project would mean for them. She did this by working with teachers and schools to help students create a Box City (see the Try It Out activity mentioned on page 146) version of the new community. This phase also involved working with city council, landowners, and citizens who had concerns about the impact of the development on their businesses and neighborhoods.

The second phase involved what Mullahey calls community building activities. The new city, named Kapolei, was just that—new. Mullahey's job was to help establish traditions that would pull people together. One way that Mullahey did this was by organizing seasonal celebrations and festivals that brought people together with food and fun. Over time, these types of activities can create a thread of tradition that helps bind people together in a common experience. And that's what community is all about.

The third way that Mullahey has been involved in the Kapolei project was in the community's new elementary school. She helped organize volunteers and round up business support in ways that brought them together to create a stronger and better school for their community.

For Mullahey, planning communities is less about building structures and more about creating good places for people to live.

Venture Capitalist

WHAT IS A VENTURE CAPITALIST?

Venture capitalists invest money in promising new or grow-ing businesses in the hopes of making more money—sooner rather than later. Three to seven years is the typical time span between payout and payoff on a venture capital project.

Venture capital arrangements are not new. One of the first known "venture capitalists" was named Isabella. She was a Spanish queen who put her money behind a certain explorer named Christopher Columbus. Needless to say, the results of this arrangement got the venture capital business off to an interesting start.

Nowadays, venture capitalists are still funding great adven-tures into uncharted territories. Instead of crossing oceans and discovering new lands, however, the discoveries made possible by venture capitalists are more likely to involve information technology, biotechnology, telecommunications, and useful new inventions. Can you imagine being there at the start of fledgling companies that later became Microsoft, FedEx, and Intel? It was venture capital that brought such innovation and technology into the mainstream of the business world.

Although you may not hear as much about these types of deals in the news, venture capitalists are also often behind projects involving construction, industrial products, and all kinds of business services. In fact, just follow the money behind any big, financially risky project, and you're likely to find a venture capitalist.

In exchange for their investment, venture capitalists generally get 30 to 50 percent ownership of the business. However, money isn't the only thing that many venture capitalists invest in these businesses. They also protect their investments by providing management expertise and other kinds of help to guide start-up companies to success.

Even though venture capital investments almost always involve lots of money—a minimum of $1 million to $2 million dollars by some accounts—the money doesn't necessarily come from the venture capitalists' own pockets. Sure, there are some wealthy individuals who use their own money to fund these types of investments. But venture capitalists are just as likely

to be extremely capable business professionals who use money from a fund put together by a group of wealthy investors, a bank, or a corporation.

Regardless of where the money comes from, venture capitalists are trained to recognize a winner. They are always on the lookout for new or growing businesses on the verge of big success. They review hundreds of business plans to find a handful that show real promise. From this handful, venture capitalists begin a process called "due diligence," which involves some very complicated research into the viability of an idea, the credibility of the people involved in the business itself, and the possibilities for success. After all this work is done, the eventual decisions, be they good or bad, are pretty much determined by gut instincts.

How does someone get the kind of good business instincts that others will trust with millions, and sometimes even billions, of dollars? Education, experience, and lots of it. A typical route to a venture capital firm starts in a good business school, earning a degree in business, finance, or economics. Next comes work experience in business, banking, or the stock market. Some people get their start working in a venture capital firm—doing anything that needs to get done and working their way up from the bottom. Any way you go, you'll need to understand how business works, the ins and outs of the stock market and other types of investing, and how to get along with the movers and shakers of the business world.

Even with the best ingredients—plenty of money, great ideas and products, and a sound management team—industry statistics indicate that up to one-third of these investments fail altogether and never pay out a dime and another third will just break even. What keeps this industry going is the final one-third, which are ventures that end up very successful and return 8 to 10 times the original investment.

Venture capital isn't a "get rich quick" sort of scheme. It's a sophisticated business run by adventurous businesspeople who aren't afraid to take a gamble on the future. It isn't for everyone. Fortunes are made—and lost—in this business.

👉 TRY IT OUT

IMAGINARY INVESTMENTS

What would it take to become a millionaire if you started today? Find out at http://www.youngmoney.com/calculators/savings_calculators/millionaire_calculator. Make a chart that shows how much you'd have to invest and how much interest you'd have to earn to make your first million by the time you are 20, 30, 40, 50, and 60.

SUCCESS IS IN THE DETAILS

Kids at your school are sick and tired of lugging those heavy backpacks around. You, being the savvy business type, see an opportunity and start making plans for a new backpack delivery service to help your classmates get their stuff from one class to another without lugging them around themselves.

Before you get started you'll want to think through all the angles and put together the beginnings of a business plan that describes the problem, identifies solutions, and includes a chart that illustrates how the service will work.

✔ CHECK IT OUT

🖱 ON THE WEB

ONLINE BUSINESS SCHOOL

Give yourself an online introduction to the world of business at some of the following Web sites:

- 💡 Learn the secrets of making money at http://www.pbs.org/wgbh/nova/moolah/.
- 💡 Find out once and for all if money grows on trees at http://www.thebritishmuseum.ac.uk/worldofmoney.
- 💡 Make it, save it, invest it with tips found at http://www.pbs.org/newshour/on2/money/money.html.
- 💡 Visit the U.S. Department of Treasury online at http://www.ustreas.gov/kids.
- 💡 Get some fun facts to show and tell at http://www.childrensmuseum.org/special_exhibits/moneyville/pop5.htm.

- Enjoy the information and activities found at the It's My Life Web site at http://pbskids.org/itsmylife/money.
- Check out your money sense at http://senseanddollars.thinkport.org.
- Make more cents at http://www.themint.org.

AT THE LIBRARY
OPPORTUNITY UNLIMITED

Once you start looking you'll find new business opportunities everywhere. Just for practice take a look at one (or more!) of the following titles. As you read, keep a list of all the different kinds of businesses that are involved in making some of these products.

Englart, Mindi. *Music CDs: From Start to Finish.* Farmington Hills, Mich.: Blackbirch, 2001.

Smith, Ryan. *Ships: From Start to Finish.* Farmington Hills, Mich.: Blackbirch, 2005.

Woods, Samuel. *Chocolate: From Start to Finish.* Farmington Hills, Mich.: Blackbirch, 2000.

———. *Recycled Paper: From Start to Finish.* Farmington Hills, Mich.: Blackbirch, 2000.

———. *Sneakers: From Start to Finish.* Farmington Hills, Mich.: Blackbirch, 1999.

SHOW ME THE MONEY

If you hope to someday manage lots of money, learn to manage the little bit you have now. Here are some helpful resources to get you going.

Bamford, Janet. *Street Wise: A Guide for Teen Investors.* New York: Bloomberg, 2000.

Bateman, Katherine. *The Young Investor: Projects and Activities for Making Your Money Grow.* Chicago: Chicago Review, 2001.

Berg, Adrianne. *The Totally Awesome Money Book for Kids.* New York: Newmarket, 2002.

Gardner, David. *The Motley Fool Investment Guide for Teens: Eight Steps to Having More Money Than Your Parents Ever Dreamed Of.* New York: Fireside, 2002.

Harman, Hollis Page. *Money Sense for Kids.* Hauppauge, N.Y.: Barrons, 2004.

Mayr, Diane. *The Everything Kids' Money Book: From Saving to Spending to Investing.* Boston: Adams Media, 2002.

🗣 WITH THE EXPERTS

National Association for Small Business Investment Companies
666 11th Street NW, Suite 750
Washington, DC 20001-4500
http://www.nasbic.org

National Venture Capital Association
1655 North Fort Myer Drive, Suite 850
Arlington, VA 22209-3114
http://www.nvca.org

GET ACQUAINTED

Bill Elsner,
Venture Capitalist

CAREER PATH

CHILDHOOD ASPIRATION:
To be a ski instructor.

FIRST JOB: Made the rounds as a young boy delivering papers, mowing lawns, and shoveling snow.

CURRENT JOB: Partner, Telecom Partners, a venture capital firm.

A ROUNDABOUT ROUTE

Bill Elsner never intended to become a venture capitalist. After trying several different majors in college, he finally settled on accounting because it would provide a good background for getting into law school. His original plan was to graduate, make a little money as an accountant, go back to law school, and become a lawyer.

But plans often change. After graduating, Elsner landed a good job as an accountant with one of the "big eight" accounting firms, and he discovered he actually liked accounting. So he forgot about law school. He became a CPA (certified public accountant) and stayed with the firm for six years.

At that point, one of Elsner's clients lured him away from the accounting firm to serve as chief financial officer for a publicly traded cable and telecommunications company. This was another good move, one Elsner enjoyed until he decided to start his own cable company specializing in international projects.

After building a thriving company that was doing business in 22 countries, Elsner took it public in an initial public offering (IPO)—for a tidy profit, of course. He stayed on to help run the company for a few years and started dabbling in the venture capital game. He invested his own money in a couple of start-up companies and, when he saw a return, liked what happened.

So when the opportunity presented itself to join forces with a partner who had started a venture capital firm by raising $15 million from a number of wealthy individuals, it was easy for Elsner to say yes. Elsner's partner had launched the company with a fund called Telecom Partners I. Together they started a second phase of the fund, called Telecom Partners II, and amassed $125 million from influential partners such as the Massachusetts Institute of Technology (MIT) and the Howard Hughes Medical Fund. Phase three of the fund, Telecom Partners III, brought in $500 million for new projects. By then, Elsner was a full-fledged venture capitalist by anyone's definition.

THE CASE OF THE SERIAL ENTREPRENEURS

Venture capitalist or not, Elsner discovered he was still an entrepreneur at heart. So he and his partner run their firm a little differently than other venture capitalists. Instead of seeking out innovative companies that other people want to start, they start their own new companies. All their companies are very specialized within the telecommunications industry.

Elsner and his partner spot a good idea, scout it out, and if it looks promising enough, put a management team in place to make a go of it. For example, Elsner discovered that in Brazil there were only 10 telephone lines per 100 people. (Compare that to 75 telephone lines per 100 people in the United States.) Elsner had a hunch that there might be a business opportunity waiting for someone who could find a way to offer alternative phone service at a lower cost. He and his partner made half a dozen trips to Brazil to investigate the situation. They ended up obtaining licenses to cover three-quarters of the country with wireless phone service. That hunch continues to pay off in a big way.

SECRETS OF SUCCESS

There are a few things Elsner would like you to know about choosing a career and making money.

1. **Money isn't everything**. Sure, it takes money to launch a business, but Elsner says that the key to success is not in the dollars but in the people. A great idea with a mediocre management team is doomed to fail. A so-so idea with a great management team will thrive. It's the quality of the people, not the quantity of dollars, that makes the difference.
2. **Money isn't everything**. Even if you make a million bucks, your career won't be worth much if you aren't enjoying yourself. From his high school days working at a ski resort and his college summers spent as a lifeguard, Elsner learned that work can be fun. Looking forward to going to work every day is much more important to him than making lots of money.

3. **Money isn't everything.** Elsner urges anyone who is planning to make money the focal point of his or her career to reconsider. He says you'll find more success if you figure out what you're good at and then do a good job. The quality of your work will take you places you never thought possible.

MAKE A DETOUR THAT ADDS UP!

Follow the numbers to more interesting career options. Make sure to find work you really enjoy—something that you believe in and will make you glad to get out of bed each morning. Find your passion and let it lead you to your future—and your fortune.

THE BIG PAYOFF
Some jobs typically associated with nice paychecks include:

actuaries

aeronautical engineers and astronautical engineers

aircraft pilots and flight engineers

chemical engineers

chiropractors
dentists
education administrators
electrical and electronic
  engineers
engineering, math, and natural
  science managers
farm and home management
  advisors
finanacial managers

general managers and top
  executives
industrial engineers
lawyers
medical scientists
mining engineers
nuclear engineers
optometrists
pharmacists
physical therapists

A CAREER IN MONEY

Want to make good money for your work? The financial world is a good place to be.

auditor
benefits officer
certified financial analyst
commercial banker
commodities broker
commodities risk manager
corporate financial analyst
credit manager
financial planner
foreign exchange
  representative

investment analyst
investment manager
investor relations officer
loan officer
market maker
mortgage broker
mutual fund manager
securities analyst
stockbroker

A HIGH-TECH WORLD

Remember that math drives the high-tech world in which we live. These careers blend math with computer skills.

artificial intelligence specialist
computer analyst
computer-aided design (CAD)
  specialist
computer engineer

computer scientist
cryptanalyst
operations manager
operations research analyst
telecommunications technician

THE DYNAMIC DUO: MATH AND SCIENCE

The following careers combine math with science.

agronomist

conservationist

astronomer
astrophysicist
biologist
biomedical engineer
chemist
climatologist

ecologist
geodesist
geologist
hydrologist
meteorologist
physicist

ENGINEERING: AN EXCITING CAREER

Engineers are at the forefront of all kinds of discovery, and engineering careers are based on many interests, including math.

aerospace engineer
agricultural engineer
automotive engineer
biomedical engineer
ceramic engineer
computer engineer
environmental engineer
industrial engineer

mechanical engineer
metallurgy engineer
mining engineer
naval engineer
nuclear engineer
petroleum engineer
robotics engineer

SOME HEALTH-MINDED CHOICES

A solid math background is essential for success in all these medical professions.

chiropractor
clinical lab technician
dental hygienist
dentist
health administrator
nurse

optician
optometrist
physical therapist
physician
respiratory therapist
surgeon

THE NUMBERS BUSINESS

Making sure the numbers add up in the business world is at the heart of these careers.

accountant
auditor
demographer
estimator
financial analyst
insurance underwriter

labor negotiator
market analyst
printer
real estate appraiser
zoning inspector

DON'T STOP NOW!

GO FOR IT!

It's been a fast-paced trip so far. Take a break, regroup, and look at all the progress you've made.

1st Stop: Discover
You discovered some personal interests and natural abilities that you can start building a career around.

2nd Stop: Explore
You've explored an exciting array of career opportunities in these fields. You're now aware that your career can involve either a specialized area with many educational require-ments or it can involve a practical application of skills with a minimum of training and experience.

At this point, you've found a couple careers that make you wonder "Is this a good option for me?" Now it's time to put it all together and make an informed, intelligent choice. It's time to get a sense of what it might be like to have a job like the one(s) you're considering. In other words, it's time to move on to step three and do a little experiment-ing with success.

3rd Stop: Experiment

By the time you finish this section, you'll have reached one of three points in the career planning process.

1. **Green light!** You found it. No need to look any further. This is the career for you. (This may happen to a lucky few. Don't worry if it hasn't happened yet for you. This whole process is about exploring options, experimenting with ideas, and, eventually, making the best choice for you.)

2. **Yellow light!** Close but not quite. You seem to be on the right path, but you haven't nailed things down for sure. (This is where many people your age end up, and it's a good place to be. You've learned what it takes to really check things out. Hang in there. Your time will come.)

3. **Red light!** Whoa! No doubt about it, this career just isn't for you. (Congratulations! Aren't you glad you found out now and not after you'd spent four years in college preparing for this career? Your next stop: Make a U-turn and start this process over with another career.)

Here's a sneak peek at what you'll be doing in the next section.

☼ First, you'll pick a favorite career idea (or two or three).
☼ Second, you'll link up with a whole world of great information about that career on the Internet (it's easier than you think).
☼ Third, you'll snoop around the library to find answers to the top 10 things you've just got to know about your future career.
☼ Fourth, you'll either write a letter or use the Internet to request information from a professional organization associated with this career.
☼ Fifth, you'll chat on the phone to conduct a telephone interview.

After all that you'll (finally!) be ready to put it all together in your very own Career Ideas for Kids career profile (see page 178).

Hang on to your hats and get ready to make tracks!

#1 NARROW DOWN YOUR CHOICES

You've been introduced to quite a few math- and money-related career ideas. You may also have some ideas of your own to add. Which ones appeal to you the most?

Write your top three choices in the spaces below. (Sorry if this is starting to sound like a broken record, but . . . if this book does not belong to you, write your responses on a separate sheet of paper.)

1. _____

2. _____

3. _____

#2 SURF THE NET

With the Internet, you have a world of information at your fingertips. The Internet has something for everyone, and it's getting easier to access all the time. An increasing number of libraries and schools are offering access to the Internet on their computers, or you may have a computer at home.

A typical career search will land everything from the latest news on developments in the field and course notes from universities to museum exhibits, interactive games, educational activities, and more. You just can't beat the timeliness or the variety of information available on the Web.

One of the easiest ways to track down this information is to use an Internet search engine, such as Yahoo! Simply type the topic you are looking for, and in a matter of seconds you'll have a list of options from around the world. For instance, if you are looking for information about companies that make candy, use the words "candy manufacturer" to start your search. It's fun to browse—you never know what you'll come up with.

Before you link up, keep in mind that many of these sites are geared toward professionals who are already working in a particular field. Some of the sites can get pretty technical. Just use the experience as a chance to nose around the field, hang out with the people who are tops in the field, and think about whether or not you'd like to be involved in a profession like that.

Specific sites to look for are the following:

Professional associations. Find out about what's happening in the field, conferences, journals, and other helpful tidbits.

Schools that specialize in this area. Many include research tools, introductory courses, and all kinds of interesting information.

Government agencies. Quite a few are going high-tech with lots of helpful resources.

Web sites hosted by experts in the field (this seems to be a popular hobby among many professionals). These Web sites are often as entertaining as they are informative.

If you're not sure where to go, just start clicking around. Sites often link to other sites. You may want to jot down notes about favorite sites. Sometimes you can even print information that isn't copyright protected; try the print option and see what happens.

Be prepared: Surfing the Internet can be an addicting habit! There is so much awesome information. It's a fun way to focus on your future.

Write the addresses of the three best Web sites that you find during your search in the space below (or on a separate sheet of paper if this book does not belong to you).

1. _____
2. _____
3. _____

#3 SNOOP AT THE LIBRARY

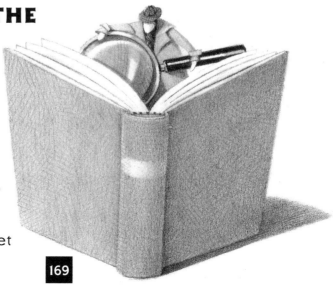

Take your list of favorite career ideas, a notebook, and a helpful adult with you to the library. When you get there, go to the reference section and ask the librarian to help you find books about careers. Most libraries will have at least one set

of career encyclopedias. Some of the larger libraries may also have career information on CD-ROM.

Gather all the information you can and use it to answer the following questions in your notebook about each of the careers on your list. Make sure to ask for help if you get stuck.

TOP 10 THINGS YOU NEED TO KNOW ABOUT YOUR CAREER

1. What is the purpose of this job?

2. What kind of place is this type of work usually done in? For example, would I work mostly in a busy office, outdoors, or in a laboratory?

3. What kind of time is required to do this job? For instance, is the job usually performed during regular daytime business hours or do people work various shifts around the clock?

4. What kinds of tools are used to do this job?

5. In what ways does this job involve working with other people?

6. What kind of preparation does a person need to qualify for this job?

7. What kinds of skills and abilities are needed to be successful in this type of work?

_____

8. What's a typical day on the job like?

_____

_____

9. How much money can I expect to earn as a beginner?

_____

10. What kind of classes do I need to take in high school to get ready for this type of work?

_____

#4 GET IN TOUCH WITH THE EXPERTS

One of the best places to find information about a particular career is a professional organization devoted especially to that career. After all, these organizations are full of the best and the brightest professionals working in that particular field. Who could possibly know more about how the work gets done? There are more than 450,000 organizations in the United States, so there is bound to be an association related to just about any career you can possibly imagine.

There are a couple ways you can find these organizations:

1. Look at the "Check It Out—With the Experts" list following a career you found especially interesting in the Take A Trip! section of this book.

2. Go online and use your favorite search engine (such as http://www.google.com or http://yahoo.com) to find professional associations related to a career you are

interested in. You might use the name of the career, plus the words "professional association" to start your search. You're likely to find lots of useful information online, so keep looking until you hit pay dirt.

3. Go to the reference section of your public library and ask the librarian to help you find a specific type of association in a reference book called *Encyclopedia of Associations* (Farmington Hills, Mich.: Thomson Gale) Or, if your library has access to it, the librarian may suggest using an online database called *Associations Unlimited* (Farmington Hills, Mich.: Thomson Gale).

Once you've tracked down a likely source of information, there are two ways to get in touch with a professional organization.

1. Send an e-mail.

Most organizations include a "contact us" button on their Web sites. Sometimes this e-mail is directed to a webmaster or a customer service representative. An e-mail request might look something like this:

Subject: Request for Information
Date: 2/1/2008 3:18:41 PM Eastern Standard Time
From: janedoe@mycomputer.com
To: webmaster@candyloversassociation.org

I am a fifth-grade student, and I am interested in learning more about careers for candy lovers. Would you please send me any information you have about what people do in your industry?

Thank you very much.
Jane Doe

2. Write a letter requesting information.

Your letter should be either typed on a computer or written in your best handwriting. It should include the date, the complete address of the organization you are contacting, a salutation or greeting, a brief

description of your request, and a signature. Make sure to include an address where the organization can reach you with a reply. Something like the following letter would work just fine.

Dear Sir or Madam:

I am a fifth-grade student, and I would like to learn more about what it is like to work in the candy lover profession. Would you please send me information about careers? My address is 456 Main Street, Anytown, USA 54321.

Thank you very much.

Sincerely,
Jane Doe

Write the names and addresses of the professional organizations you discover on a separate sheet of paper.

#5 CHAT ON THE PHONE

Talking to a seasoned professional—someone who experiences the job day in and day out—can be a great way to get the inside story on what a career is all about. Fortunately for you, the experts in any career field can be as close as the nearest telephone.

Sure, it can be a bit scary calling up an adult whom you don't know. But two things are in your favor:

1. They can't see you. The worst thing they can do is hang up on you, so just relax and enjoy the conversation.

2. They'll probably be happy to talk to you about their job. In fact, most people will be flattered that you've called. If you happen to contact someone who seems reluctant to talk, thank them for their time and try someone else.

Here are a few pointers to help make your telephone interview a success:

💡 Mind your manners and speak clearly.
💡 Be respectful of their time and position.
💡 Be prepared with good questions and take notes as you talk.

One more common sense reminder: be careful about giving out your address and DO NOT arrange to meet anyone you don't know without your parents' supervision.

TRACKING DOWN CAREER EXPERTS

You might be wondering by now how to find someone to interview. Have no fear! It's easy if you're persistent. All you have to do is ask. Ask the right people and you'll have a great lead in no time.

A few of the people to ask and sources to turn to are:

Your parents. They may know someone (or know someone who knows someone) who has just the kind of job you're looking for.

Your friends and neighbors. You might be surprised to find out how many interesting jobs these people have when you start asking them what they (or their parents) do for a living.

Librarians. Since you've already figured out what kinds of companies employ people in your field of interest, the next step is to ask for information about local employers. Although it's a bit cumbersome to use, a big volume called *Contacts Influential* can provide this kind of information.

Professional associations. Call, e-mail, or write to the professional associations you discovered using the activity on pages 171–173 and ask for recommendations.

Chambers of commerce. The local chamber of commerce probably has a directory of employers, their specialties, and their phone numbers. Call the chamber, explain what you are looking for, and give them a chance to help their future workforce.

Newspaper and magazine articles. Find an article about the subject you are interested in. Chances are pretty good that it will mention the name of at least one expert in the field. The article probably won't include the person's phone number (that would be too easy), so you'll have to look for clues. Common clues include the name of the company that they work for, the town that they live in, and, if the person is an author, the name of their publisher. Make a few phone calls and track them down (if long distance calls are involved, make sure to get your parents' permission first).

INQUIRING KIDS WANT TO KNOW

Before you make the call, make a list of questions to ask. You'll cover more ground if you focus on using the five W's (and the H) that you've probably heard about in your creative writing classes: Who? What? Where? When? How? and Why? For example:

1. Whom do you work for?

   _____

2. What is a typical workday like for you?

   _____

3. Where can I get some on-the-job experience?

   _____

4. When did you become a _____?
(profession)

5. How much can you earn in this profession? (But remember, it's not polite to ask someone how much *he* or *she* earns.)

_____

6. Why did you choose this profession?

_____

Use a grid like the one below to keep track of the questions you ask in the boxes labeled "Q" and the answers you receive in the boxes labeled "A."

Who?	What?	Where?	When?	How?	Why?
Q	Q	Q	Q	Q	Q
A	A	A	A	A	A
Q	Q	Q	Q	Q	Q
A	A	A	A	A	A

One last suggestion: Add a professional (and very classy) touch to the interview process by following up with a thank-you note to the person who took time out of a busy schedule to talk with you.

#6 INFORMATION IS POWER

As you may have noticed, a similar pattern of information was used for each of the careers profiled in this book. Each entry included:

- ☀ a general description of the career
- ☀ Try It Out activities to give readers a chance to find out what it's really like to do each job
- ☀ a list of Web sites, library resources, and professional organizations to check for more information
- ☀ a get-acquainted interview with a professional

You may have also noticed that all the information you just gathered would fit rather nicely in a Career Ideas for Kids career profile of your own. Just fill in the blanks on the following pages to get your thoughts together (or, if this book does not belong to you, use a separate sheet of paper).

And by the way, this formula is one that you can use throughout your life to help you make fully informed career choices.

CAREER TITLE _____

WHAT IS A _____ **?**
Use career encyclopedias and other resources to write a description of this career.

SKILL SET

✔ _____
✔ _____
✔ _____

_____

_____

_____

_____

 TRY IT OUT

Write project ideas here. Ask your parents and your teacher to come up with a plan.

_____

_____

_____

_____

_____

✔ CHECK IT OUT

🖱 ON THE WEB

List Internet addresses of interesting Web sites you find.

_____

_____

_____

_____

_____

 AT THE LIBRARY

List the titles and authors of books about this career.

_____

_____

_____

_____

_____

WITH THE EXPERTS

List professional organizations where you can learn more about this profession.

_____

_____

_____

_____

_____

GET ACQUAINTED

Interview a professional in the field and summarize your findings.

_____

_____

_____

_____

_____

_____

_____

WHAT'S NEXT?

Whoa, everybody! At this point, you've put in some serious miles on your career exploration journey. Before you move on, let's put things in reverse for just a sec and take another look at some of the clues you uncovered about yourself when you completed the "Discover" activities in the Get in Gear chapter on pages 7 to 26.

The following activities will help lay the clues you learned about yourself alongside the clues you learned about a favorite career idea. The comparison will help you decide if that particular career idea is a good idea for you to pursue. It doesn't matter if a certain career sounds absolutely amazing. If it doesn't honor your skills, your interests, and your values, it's not going to work for you.

The first time you looked at these activities, they were numbered one through five as "Discover" activities. This time around they are numbered in the same order but labeled "Rediscover" activities. That's not done to confuse you (sure hope it doesn't!). Instead, it's done to drive home a very important point that this is an important process you'll want to revisit time and time again as you venture throughout your career—now and later.

First, pick the one career idea that you are most interested in at this point and write its name here (or if this book doesn't belong to you, blah, blah, blah—you know the drill by now):

_____

With that idea in mind, revisit your responses to the following Get in Gear activities and complete the following:

REDISCOVER #1:
WATCH FOR SIGNS ALONG THE WAY

Based on your responses to the statements on page 8, choose which of the following road signs best describes how you feel about your career idea:

- ⚡ Green light—Go! Go! Go! This career idea is a perfect fit!
- ⚡ Yellow light—Proceed with caution! This career idea is a good possibility, but you're not quite sure that it's the "one" just yet.
- ⚡ Stop—Hit the brakes! There's no doubt about it—this career idea is definitely not for you!

REDISCOVER #2:
RULES OF THE ROAD

Take another look at the work-values chart you made on page 16. Now use the same symbols to create a work-values chart for the career idea you are considering. After you have all the symbols in place, compare the two charts and answer these questions:

- ☼ Does your career idea's **purpose** line up with yours? Would it allow you to work in the kind of **place** you most want to work in?
- ☼ What about the **time** commitment—is it in sync with what you're hoping for?
- ☼ Does it let you work with the **tools** and the kind of **people** you most want to work with?
- ☼ And, last but not least, are you willing to do what it takes to **prepare** for a career like this?

PURPOSE	PLACE	TIME
TOOLS	PEOPLE	PREPARATION

REDISCOVER #3:
DANGEROUS DETOURS

Go back to page 16 and double-check your list of 10 careers that you hope to avoid at any cost.

Is this career on that list? ____Yes ____ No

Should it be? ____Yes ____ No

REDISCOVER #4:
ULTIMATE CAREER DESTINATION

Pull out the ultimate career destination brochure you made (as described on page 17). Use a pencil to cross through every reference to "my ideal career" and replace it with the name of the career idea you are now considering.

Is the brochure still true? _____Yes _____ No

If not, what would you change on the brochure to make it true?

REDISCOVER #5:
GET SOME DIRECTION

Quick! Think fast! What is your personal Skill Set as discovered on page 26?

Write down your top three interest areas:

1. _____

2. _____

3. _____

What three interest areas are most closely associated with your career idea?

1. _____

2. _____

3. _____

Does this career's interest areas match any of yours?
_____Yes _____ No

Now the big question: Are you headed in the right direction?

If so, here are some suggestions to keep you moving ahead:

- ☼ Keep learning all you can about this career—read, surf the Web, talk to people, and so on. In other words, keep using some of the strategies you used in the Don't Stop Now chapter on pages 165 to 179 to do all you can to make a fully informed career decision.
- ☼ Work hard in school and get good grades. What you do now counts! Your performance, your behavior, your attitude—all conspire to either propel you forward or hold you back.
- ☼ Get involved in clubs and other after-school activities to further develop your interests and skills. Whether it's student government, 4-H, or sports, these kinds of activities give you a chance to try new things and gain confidence in your abilities.

If not, here are some suggestions to help you regroup:

- ☼ Read other books in the Career Ideas for Kids series to explore options associated with your other interest areas.
- ☼ Take a variety of classes in school and get involved in different kinds of after-school activities to get a better sense of what you like and what you do well.
- ☼ Talk to your school guidance counselor about taking a career assessment test to help fine-tune your focus.
- ☼ Most of all, remember that time is on your side. Use the next few years to discover more about yourself, explore the options, and experiment with what it will take to make you succeed. Keep at it and look forward to a fantastic future!

HOORAY! YOU DID IT!

This has been quite a trip. If someone tries to tell you that this process is easy, don't believe them. Figuring out what you want to do with the rest of your life is heavy stuff, and it should be. If you don't put some thought (and some sweat and hard work) into the process, you'll get stuck with whatever comes your way.

You may not have things planned to a T. Actually, it's probably better if you don't. You'll change some of your ideas as you grow and experience new things. And, you may find an interesting detour or two along the way. That's OK.

The most important thing about beginning this process now is that you've started to dream. You've discovered that you have some unique talents and abilities to share. You've become aware of some of the ways you can use them to make a living—and perhaps make a difference in the world.

Whatever you do, don't lose sight of the hopes and dreams you've discovered. You've got your entire future ahead of you. Use it wisely.

PASSPORT TO YOUR FUTURE

Getting where you want to go requires patience, focus, and lots of hard work. It also hinges on making good choices. Following is a list of some surefire ways to give yourself the best shot at a bright future. Are you up to the challenge? Can you do it? Do you dare?

Put your initials next to each item that you absolutely promise to do.

___ ☼ Do my best in every class at school
___ ☼ Take advantage of every opportunity to get a wide variety of experiences through participation in sports, after-school activities, at my favorite place of worship, and in my community
___ ☼ Ask my parents, teachers, or other trusted adults for help when I need it
___ ☼ Stay away from drugs, alcohol, and other bad scenes that can rob me of a future before I even get there
___ ☼ Graduate from high school

SOME FUTURE DESTINATIONS

Wow! Look how far you've come! By now you should be well-equipped to discover, explore, and experiment your way to an absolutely fantastic future. To keep you headed in the right direction, this section will point you toward useful resources that provide more insight, information, and inspiration as you continue your quest to find the perfect career.

IT'S NOT JUST FOR NERDS

The school counselor's office is not just a place where teachers send troublemakers. One of its main purposes is to help students like you make the most of your educational opportunities. Most schools will have a number of useful resources, including career assessment tools (ask about the Self-Directed Search Career Explorer or the COPS Interest

Inventory—these are especially useful assessments for people your age). They may also have a stash of books, videos, and other helpful materials.

Make sure no one's looking and sneak into your school counseling office to get some expert advice!

AWESOME INTERNET CAREER RESOURCES

Your parents will be green with envy when they see all the career planning resources you have at your fingertips. Get ready to hear them whine, "But they didn't have all this stuff when I was a kid." Make the most of these cyberspace opportunities.

☼ **Adventures in Education**
http://adventuresineducation.org/middleschool
Here you'll find some useful tools to make the most of your education—starting now. Make sure to watch "The Great College Mystery," an online animation featuring Dr. Ed.

☼ **America's Career InfoNet**
http://www.acinet.org
Career sites don't get any bigger than this one! Compliments of the U.S. Department of Labor, and a chunk of your parent's tax dollars, you'll find all kinds of information about what people do, how much money they make, and where they work. Although it's mostly geared toward adults, you may want to take a look at some of the videos (the site has links to more than 450!) that show people at work.

☼ **ASVAB Career Exploration Program**
http://www.asvabprogram.com
This site may prove especially useful as you continue to think through various options. It includes sections

for students to learn about themselves, to explore careers, and to plan for their futures.

☼ Career Voyages
http://www.careervoyages.gov
This site will be especially helpful to you as you get a little older. It offers four paths to get you started: "Where do I start?" "Which industries are growing?" "How do I qualify and get a job?" and "Does education pay? How do I pay?" However, it also includes a special section especially for elementary school students. Just click the button that says "Still in elementary school?" or go to http://www.careervoyages.gov/students-elementary.cfm.

☼ Job Profiles
http://jobprofiles.org
This site presents the personal side of work with profiles of people working in jobs associated with agriculture and nature, arts and sports, business and communications, construction and manufacturing, education and science, government, health and social services, retail and wholesale, and other industries.

☼ Major and Careers Central
http://www.collegeboard.com/csearch/majors_careers
This site is hosted by the College Board (the organization responsible for a very important test called the SAT, which you're likely to encounter if you plan to go to college). It includes helpful information about how different kinds of subjects you can study in college can prepare you for specific types of jobs.

☼ Mapping Your Future
http://mapping-your-future.org/MHSS

This site provides strategies and resources for students as they progress through middle school and high school.

☼ My Cool Career
http://www.mycoolcareer.com
This site is where you can take free online self-assessment quizzes, explore your dreams, and listen to people with interesting jobs talk about their work.

☼ O*NET Online
http://online.onetcenter.org
This U.S. Department of Labor site provides comprehensive information about hundreds of important occupations. Although you may need to ask a parent or teacher to help you figure out how to use the system, it can be a good source of digging for nitty-gritty details about a specific type of job. For instance, each profile includes a description of the skills, abilities, and special knowledge needed to perform each job.

☼ Think College Early
http://www.ed.gov/students/prep/college
thinkcollege/early/edlite-tcehome.html
Even though you almost need a college degree just to type the Web address for this U.S. Department of Education site, it contains some really cool career information and helps you think about how college might fit into your future plans.

☼ What Interests You?
http://www.bls.gov/k12
This Bureau of Labor Statistics site is geared toward students. It lets you explore careers by interests such as reading, building and fixing things, managing money, helping people, and more.

JOIN THE CLUB

Once you've completed eighth grade, you are eligible to check out local opportunities to participate in Learning for Life's career education programs. Some communities offer Explorer posts that sponsor activities with students interested in industries that include the arts and humanities, aviation, business, communications, engineering, fire service, health, law enforcement, law and government, science, skilled trades, or social services. To find a local office, go to http://www.learning-for-life.org/exploring/main.html and type your zip code.

Until then, you can go online and play *Life Choices*, a really fun and challenging game where you get one of five virtual jobs at http://www.learning-for-life.org/games/LCSH/index.html.

MORE CAREER BOOKS ESPECIALLY FOR KIDS

It's especially important that people your age find out all they can about as many different careers as they can. Books like the ones listed below can introduce all kinds of interesting ideas that you might not encounter in your everyday life.

Greenfeld, Barbara C., and Robert A. Weinstein. *The Kids' College Almanac: A First Look at College.* 3d ed. Indianapolis, Ind.: JIST Works, 2005.
Young Person's Occupational Outlook Handbook. Indianapolis, Ind.: JIST Works, 2005.

Following are brief descriptions of several series of books geared especially toward kids like you. To find copies of these books, ask your school or public librarian to help you search the library computer system using the name of the series.

Career Connections (published by UXL)

This extensive series features information and illustrations about jobs of interest to people interested in art and design, entrepreneurship, food, government and law, history, math and computers, and the performing arts as well as those who want to work with their hands or with living things.

Career Ideas for Kids (written by Diane Lindsey Reeves, published by Ferguson)

This series of interactive career exploration books features 10 different titles for kids who like adventure and travel, animals and nature, art, computers, math and money, music and dance, science, sports, talking, and writing.

Careers Without College (published by Peterson's)

These books offer a look at options available to those who prefer to find jobs that do not require a college degree and include titles focusing on cars, computers, fashion, fitness, health care, and music.

Cool Careers (published by Rosen Publishing)

Each title in this series focuses on a cutting-edge occupation such as computer animator, hardware engineer, multimedia and new media developer, video game designer, Web entrepreneur, and webmaster.

Discovering Careers for Your Future (published by Ferguson)

This series includes a wide range of titles that include those that focus on adventure, art, construction, fashion, film, history, nature, publishing, and radio and television.

Risky Business (written by Keith Elliot Greenberg, published by Blackbirch Press)

These books feature stories about people with adventurous types of jobs and include titles about a bomb squad officer, disease detective, marine biologist, photojournalist, rodeo clown, smoke jumper, storm chaser, stunt woman, test pilot, and wildlife special agent.

HEAVY-DUTY RESOURCES

Career encyclopedias provide general information about a lot of professions and can be a great place to start a career search. Those listed here are easy to use and provide useful information about nearly a zillion different jobs. Look for them in the reference section of your local library.

Career Discovery Encyclopedia, 6th ed. New York: Ferguson, 2006.

Careers for the 21st Century. Farmington Hills, Mich.: Lucent Books, 2002.

Children's Dictionary of Occupations. Princeton, N.J.: Cambridge Educational, 2004.

Encyclopedia of Career and Vocational Guidance. New York: Ferguson, 2005.

Farr, Michael, and Laurence Shatkin. *Enhanced Occupational Outlook Handbook.* 6th ed. Indianapolis, Ind.: JIST Works, 2006.

Occupational Outlook Handbook. Washington, D.C.: U.S. Government Printing Office, 2006.

FINDING PLACES TO WORK

Even though you probably aren't quite yet in the market for a real job, you can learn a lot about the kinds of jobs you might find if you were looking by visiting some of the most popular job-hunting sites on the Internet. Two particularly good ones to investigate are America's Job Bank (http://www.ajb.org) and Monster (http://www.monster.com).

INDEX

Page numbers in **boldface** indicate main articles. Page numbers in *italics* indicate photographs.